PRAISE FOR **BUILI**

MW00438523

Ted Travis has written a moving book on urban youth. By examining youth ministry through the lens of Christian community development, he has brought to light what the church can and should be doing to bring hope and new life to youth in our cities.

Years ago, I shared my burden concerning youth with Ted: How do we build incentive in these kids? How do we induce change from within? *Building Cathedrals* gives a powerful response to that question.

I agree with Ted: It is time to weave what he calls transformational discipleship into the fabric of youth ministry. I encourage pastors, youth leaders and people concerned about the state of our youth in the city to read this book.

Dr. John Perkins
Co-founder, Christian Community Development Association
Author, *Let Justice Roll Down*

It is my contention that the missional field of youth culture in the U.S. is an ever-increasing multi-ethnic and metropolitan reality. We can no longer afford to marginalize urban youth ministry, for it is becoming more and more the main stream of youth ministry. Ted Travis offers deep insight into understanding a model of transformational ministry to at-risk urban youth that can assist in rethinking youth ministry in a broad way into the future. This is a much-needed resource.

Efrem Smith
President and CEO, World Impact
Author, *The Post-Black and Post-White Church*

Readers will learn a great deal from Ted Travis's rich urban ministry experience. His insights about adolescents, community engagement and ministry are a vast ocean of information that challenges us to reexamine our theological and ministerial assumptions about urban youth work. And his gift of storytelling—from programmatic frustrations to personal sharing to leadership strategies—paints a beautiful and very human portrait providing the backdrop from which much of his sage advice flows.

Fernando Arzola Jr., Ph.D.
Dean of Arts and Sciences, Nyack College
Author, *Toward a Prophetic Youth Ministry: Theory and Praxis in Urban Context*

Ted Travis has written a book that has been long overdue! He has thought intently, theologically, philosophically and practically about the depths of what it means to empower our youth in the urban community through a transformational discipleship approach to urban youth development. If you just started ministry to youth, this is a mandatory read to take you in the right direction with your work with young people; and sadly, if you are a veteran, it might just be the book to bring you back into focus. *Trust ya boy*, get this book and study it.

Pastor Phil Jackson, M.Div.

John Perkins Scholar
Associate Pastor of LCC and Lead Pastor of The House
Founder and ED of The Firehouse Community Art Center

It is rare to find a relevant guide for developing young leaders that is rooted in the urban context and that is both biblical and practical.

In his new book, *Building Cathedrals*, my good friend and long-time CCDA leader and board member has given us an important resource to help engage in deep discipleship among our youth.

Thanks, Ted, for sharing your wisdom with a new generation of youth workers!

Noel Castellanos

President and CEO, Christian Community Development Association
Author, *Where the Cross Meets the Street: What Happens to the Neighborhood When God Is at the Center*

It is rare when a book comes along that both summarizes a person's—and in this case, a couple's—life and ministry and also paves the way for others to learn from their years of faithful and powerful ministry. I have had the privilege to know Ted Travis for nearly three decades, and he is among the brightest, most committed and creative leaders I have been around. In *Building Cathedrals*, Ted unpacks in clear and practical language the why and what of long-term effective urban youth ministry. He has lived what he writes, and he brings a ministry longevity and reality to this book that not only lends credibility but also offers hope. I am so grateful for Ted and Shelly—for their ministry and faithfulness and consistency, and now for the gift of this book, helping the world to learn from the work, sacrifice and genuine love that this family has given to the people of Denver.

Chap Clark, PhD

Professor of Youth, Family, and Culture
Fuller Theological Seminary
Author, *Hurt 2.0: Inside the World of Today's Teenagers*

TED TRAVIS

BUILDING
CATHEDRALS

URBAN YOUTH
DISCIPLESHIP THAT WORKS

NEIGHBORHOOD MINISTRIES/TDI

From Neighborhood Ministries
Denver, Colorado
www.tdinitiative.org
Printed in the U.S.A.

ISBN: 978-0-9966037-0-6

Library of Congress Cataloging-in-Publication Data
(Applied for)

14 15 16 17 18 19 20 | 10 9 8 7 6 5 4 3 2 1

To Shelly: life partner, best friend,
God's greatest gift to me.
My life—and the lives of many in the urban
community—is richer because of you.

CONTENTS

FOREWORD

"What is the most serious concern in the inner city?" a friend recently asked me.

It was not a difficult question to answer. Without hesitation, I responded: "The African-American male."

From infancy, young black men who live in urban poverty learn that survival, not achievement, is their assigned role. Immediate gratification, respect earned by bold confrontation, blatant disregard for society's rules—such are the values that the street teaches them early on. Formal education makes little sense. School is for women who can get meager jobs—who still hold out hope for their offspring. Prison is the finishing school that completes a street education; it is a rite of passage for young black men. Sexual conquest with multiple women is a sign of manliness, as marriage and parental support are hardly options in the absence of stable employment. Guns, drugs, stealth and violence characterize the economy that these men deal in. Little wonder that their death rate is the highest—and their achievement rate the lowest—among poverty populations in this country.

Were there an endangered species list for humans, the urban African-American male would be receiving special government protection. Instead, they are viewed by society as pariahs—predators to be isolated and, when necessary, hunted down, trapped, caged or killed.

I hasten to point out, however, that the permanent underclass where the endangered black male survives is only one small segment of African-American culture. The larger black population has done quite well in our country over the past several decades.

Pulitzer Prize-winning *Washington Post* writer Eugene Robinson, in his penetrating book *Disintegration: The Splintering of Black America*, describes four distinct black Americas. The large middle-class majority—the Mainstream—is well-educated, well-employed and has a full ownership stake in American society. The ambitious Emergents are those of mixed-race heritage and the more recent black immigrants who view the United States as a land of unparalleled opportunity and have little connection to our historic civil rights struggle. The Transcendent Elite (the Oprahs, the Cosbys, the Obamas) have gained such wealth, power and influence "that even white folks have to genuflect." And then there are the Abandoned—the left-behind minority "with less hope of escaping poverty and dysfunction than at any time since Reconstruction's crushing end."[1]

The "black agenda" of the civil rights era, with its unified interests and needs, has largely dissipated. Much like Gettysburg and Bull Run, the battlefields where war was waged over racial segregation of housing, education and jobs are but silent reminders of past struggles. Post-WWII prosperity and civil rights achievements opened wide for black Americans' access to "the American Dream."

And most pursued it. Most.

But while the hopeful and ambitious enrolled in better schools, bought suburban homes and climbed the economic ladder, their lesser skilled neighbors found it difficult to follow. Once-reliable paths out of poverty became blocked as manufacturing jobs shipped overseas and public education imploded. As the economic gap widened, so too did the social distance. A splintering of black America took place as once-unified communities moved apart, separating by "demography, geography, and psychology."[2]

Today, the social canyons that isolate the Abandoned from the rest of society are nearly impassable. The occasional escapee—a brilliant student or an outstanding athlete—who by steely determination or saintly support is able to make the crossing, will of necessity sever ties with the dysfunction of the 'hood and disappear into the Mainstream. The rising star, so bright with promise, soon disappears from sight, leaving the ghetto an even darker place—another reminder that it is the haunt for survivors, not achievers.

These days there is little patience with the black, inner-city male or the underclass world that he roams. Public interest, though temporarily sparked by Ferguson and Baltimore, will soon move on to other issues. A once-sympathetic nation has hardened its heart against what is widely considered (though seldom so-labeled out loud) an irresponsible residue who have, for reasons known only to them, rejected the opportunities available to every other American.

So long as the violence remains black-on-black, so long as the crack houses stay in the ghetto, there will be no public outcry. And certainly no sympathy. The prevailing attitude in the dominant culture is head-wagging disgust: *If this rogue culture chooses to remain hostile to society and prey shamelessly on the vulnerable, then they deserve what they get.* At least, this is the prevailing attitude of most white Americans.

We see the struggles of the urban African-American community as their problem, not ours. But it *is* our problem, and its implications are far-reaching. Budget-conscious citizens are rightfully concerned about the disproportionate amount of tax dollars spent on prisons and law enforcement to contain the problem. Teachers and social workers despair over the seeming futility of their dedicated efforts to inspire hope. Urban ministries feature glowing success stories of transformed lives, but seldom tell of the discouraging setbacks or of watching helplessly as their converts get pulled back into the undertow of the streets.

A civilized society cannot indefinitely close its eyes to such brokenness, but what are we to do? If the billions poured into the war on poverty didn't work, if the historic civil rights achievements failed to provide a way out, if our evangelism blitzes and charitable ministries haven't effected perceptible change, what is left for us to try? Recent cases of police violence may galvanize activists around the issue of profiling experienced by nearly all African Americans regardless of social status, but as soon as funds are allocated for additional police training and vest cameras become standard issue, the low-income black community will fade once again from the news.

These factors underscore the importance of this book. *Building Cathedrals* stands out as a unique, powerfully written text that addresses head-on the most neglected sector of our society. Its author is bold enough to believe that the Church can be stirred from its complacency to take on what is clearly the most intractable urban issue of our time.

Ted Travis knows the domain of the Abandoned. While most capable urban youth workers, after a few years in the trenches, move on to "better" positions as pastors and agency executives, Ted has intentionally stayed behind. For decades. He is one of those rare urban visionaries who has never lost his calling or compassion for inner-city youth. The model he has lived and the insights he has gained are now being offered to the broader Christian community in the hopes that renewed interest will be sparked—that there will be a fresh vision in the Church for reclaiming a lost generation.

No one understands the issues and the risks involved in pursuing this vision better than Ted does. In *Building Cathedrals*, he delivers a reality-tested guidebook to those who have the courage and commitment to take on what is arguably the most difficult ministry challenge of our day.

Robert Lupton

Notes

1. Eugene Robinson, *Disintegration: The Splintering of Black America* (New York: Anchor Books, 2011), p. 5.
2. Ibid.

ACKNOWLEDGMENTS

This book was five years in the making.

I wish to thank Steven Lawson, who five years ago looked at an early manuscript and said bluntly, "This looks like something that was attached to a dissertation." (It was!) But he never gave up on me, and later agreed to serve as project manager. My heartfelt thanks go out to Alexis Spencer-Byers and Robert Williams, the professionals Steven recruited, for their excellent work as copy editor and graphic designer.

Praise God for cheerleaders! I especially thank Gordon England, Robert Mossman, George Law and David Bartlett, dear friends who provided constant and steady encouragement to finish the book. And I especially thank Bob Lupton, both for his insightful forward and for the incredible love and support he has given Shelly and me over the years.

Praise God for those who inspire! Glen, Jimmy, Paulette, Raquel—they have been an inspiration to me, and I pray their stories will inspire countless other urban youth to follow in their footsteps. I must give a special shout-out to the men of Hope House on the west side of Chicago. They allowed me to see and speak to their God-given potential by studying the Scriptures together weekly for four years. They helped me to refine a transforming approach to reaching urban young people. For that I am grateful.

I am indebted to the Christian Community Development Association for the rich fellowship it has provided with ministry leaders across the nation and around the world. I especially thank John and Vera Mae Perkins. God has used them mightily in my life. Shelly and I can think of no better role models for the work God has called us to do. For that we say, "Thank you!"

Finally, this project could not have been completed without the strong support of my best friend and first reader, Shelly. In my most difficult moments, she kept me going. Thank you, my love, for your faithfulness.

INTRODUCTION

The urban world seems to be on a downward spiral. In the wake of recent confrontations between black youth and police authorities, tensions have reached a fever pitch.

There is plenty of blame to go around. A few bad apples can taint the image of an entire group, be it law enforcement or city youth. Aspersion casting aside, one glaring truth remains: Urban youth are in trouble.

Many of my activist friends tirelessly address the ill effects of a broken justice system and the motivations behind the pent-up anger and seemingly mindless destruction now being unleashed on our cities. My thoughts, however, turn to the young people who died as a result of these confrontations—and to their peers who remain seriously at risk. Where were we, the church, earlier in their lives? How did we influence them? What role in their upbringing should the church embrace? What can we do to help steer at-risk youth toward a better life?

An event took place during a recent riot in Baltimore that captured national attention: A mother spotted her son embedded in a group of rioters. Near hysteria, she grabbed and slapped him, screaming expletives as she pulled him away from the mob. Later she told a reporter: "Is he a perfect son? No. But he's mine."

Why did the video of this event go viral? The media applauded the mother for her actions. Most viewers saw an impassioned mom squashing destructive behavior—and wished that more would do the same. The mother saw her son, the child she loves, doing something that was destructive to himself as well as to others. In desperation, she intervened to save him.

"I praise you because I am fearfully and wonderfully made," says the psalmist (Psalm 139:14). Far too many onlookers view urban youth as thugs-in-the-making. Not so their mothers. Loving moms see their children as cathedrals-at-risk. Beneath the harsh exterior lies something beautiful and unique, endangered yet worth saving.

On this point God agrees. I can almost hear Him saying to that distraught mother, "No, he is Mine." Jesus commissioned His followers to make a thrust among the nations that would have as its focus the transformation of people's lives (see Matthew 28:19). Such a thrust is desperately needed among youth in our urban centers today.

That is the purpose of this book: to introduce to those serving youth in our city centers a transformational discipleship approach to urban youth development. (For those readers who are not personally involved in urban youth ministry, my hope is that the material shared here will provide insight into the extreme challenges facing our youth leaders today—and the responsibility the church has to support their efforts to bring about the transformation of young lives.)

I have made my home in at-risk communities for over 35 years. I have sought to engage youth not from the limited vantage point of an outsider, but rather with the more intimate awareness and concern held by a parent. And I have constantly been reminded that as loving as a parent's perspective is, it pales before the love God has for His image-bearers.

In this lies our hope. It is time to see what God sees—and respond accordingly. The harshness of the urban landscape does not diminish the mandate to join in the cathedral-building business. This book offers a glimpse of what such a ministry can look like.

The Need

Chapter 1

BEGINNINGS

*In 1993, the year of Denver's "summer of violence," there were
74 homicides in the city. The year before, there had been 95.
The year after, there were 81 murders—and 81 again the year after that.
So in raw numbers, the "summer of violence" was an exaggeration.
In raw fear, it wasn't. . . . Nearly half the murders that year—36 of 74—
were of teenagers. Many of them were drive-by shootings.
[Then-Governor Roy] Romer called the senselessness of such
acts "an abandoning of our moral code."*[1]

In the fall of 1979, I moved into Denver's Five Points area, which some historians have called the Harlem of the West. The juvenile court had referred into my care a neighborhood kid who happened to be a leader—he was the best thief on his block. Through him I began meeting with 15 high school-aged youth at my house. Our weekly meetings consisted of food, fun and a "rap session" where we would talk about issues impacting their lives, and I would try to present, in terms they could understand, God's perspective on life.

I launched Neighborhood Ministries as a youth outreach ministry in the fall of 1980 and married the love of my life, Shelly, in 1981. The year after that, we were introduced to the founder of Christian community development, John Perkins. He quickly became a mentor and life-long friend. His books laying out his philosophy and ministry experience affirmed ideas that were already stirring my soul. I began what became a 30-year journey: applying John's Christian community development concepts to youth ministry.

As a novice at leading a Christian organization, I had a lot of learning to do. The breadth of my ignorance was revealed every time I exclaimed: "I don't know what 'administration' is, but I know it will put a hurtin' on you if you don't do it!"

I wanted to build a ministry that would last, so I researched how organizations work. Studying Charles Hobbs's Time Power materials led to crafting a set of unifying principles and core values that would define our organization. Later Verley Sangster, then National Director for Urban Young Life, introduced us to Bobb Biehl's Masterplanning materials. While Denver Seminary prepared me to think theologically, Masterplanning provided concepts and processes that were crucial to lead a Christian organization.

Because my interests centered on youth development, grasping the what and how-to of youth development became a defining quest. In particular, my staff and I pondered motivation: how a ministry might foster within youth incentives to learn and grow.

Above all we studied youth themselves. We taught them and they taught us. One of our early teachers was a young man named Jimmy.

A Lesson from Jimmy

Our ministry first encountered Jimmy when he was a sophomore in high school. He was an O.G. (Original Gangster). He, along with a few other members of his family, had helped transplant the Crips gang from Compton (Los Angeles) to northeast Denver.

Some of Jimmy's neighbors and childhood friends were involved with our weekly youth club program, and Jimmy often tagged along. The following summer, Jimmy attended summer camp, where he prayed to receive Christ. Over the next few years, his attendance waned, and for a while we lost track of him. But then he reappeared, expressing a strong desire to get married (to a Christian girl he had met at camp), grow in his faith, and go into the ministry. So I led him and his girlfriend, Andrea, through premarital counseling, performed their wedding, and brought him onto the Neighborhood Ministries staff.

Jimmy was a Pied Piper with kids; they flocked to him, and he loved sharing the gospel with them. But, like many charismatic youth leaders, his organizational skills were lacking. An older staff member and trusted advisor (coincidentally also named Jim) and I debated whether we should steer Jimmy in the direction of ministry or toward a less demanding vocation.

"He has skills as a carpenter," Jim would say. "Let him be a carpenter."

"But what if this is an expression of what God *really* wants to do with his life?" I would counter.

The crucible of inner-city life often forces youth to focus not on their potential but on the pragmatics of survival. The simple fact of Jimmy's aspiration toward vocational ministry made him an exception to that trend. "If this ministry desire is a reflection of God's imprint," I concluded, "then I'm obligated as a Christian leader to guide him in that direction."

So I set out to teach Jimmy everything I knew about leading a nonprofit Christian ministry. He accompanied me to meetings with church mission boards. I showed him our financial systems and taught him about fundraising. I created opportunities for him to speak in churches, and I encouraged those who supported us to support him. His leadership capacities grew.

Then, in 1995, the Christian Community Development Association (a group comprised of various churches, ministries and individuals committed to the principles of Christian community development pioneered by John Perkins) held its national conference in Denver. Jimmy and I were awarded the Tom Skinner Leadership Award, in recognition of outstanding leadership development. The national exposure led to his being recruited by another ministry. The following year, Jimmy and his family moved to Dallas. A year later, he left that ministry and planted his own work, serving youth in a small under-resourced neighborhood in south Dallas.

When Jimmy left Denver, we both thought it was time for him to move on. Ours was a father/son kind of relationship, and the son needed to leave the nest and spread his wings. But we also felt that I had failed him in the area of discipleship. Our study times had been sporadic at best. I felt pangs of regret until Jimmy shared something about his first year as a ministry founder and director:

> I left Denver disappointed that you had not discipled me. But when I became a ministry director, I found myself asking almost daily: "What would Ted do in this situation?" I began to remember everything you ever taught me.

Jimmy taught us the importance of what I have come to see as an apprentice (i.e., learning while doing) approach to youth development. He also taught us to look beyond the damaging influence of the 'hood and focus on animating—bringing to life—a young person's divine imprint—God's unique design.

To this day, Jimmy continues to minister among youth, building on the foundation we laid together during his time as an apprentice.

Perspectives on Leadership

These discoveries—an apprentice approach and a focus on the divine imprint—led to new perspectives on leadership. What does leadership look like in the youth ministry context?

Jesus spoke of leadership as servanthood:

> Jesus called them together and said, "You know that those who are regarded as rulers of the Gentiles lord it

over them, and their high officials exercise authority over them. Not so with you. Instead, whoever wants to become great among you must be your servant, and whoever wants to be first must be slave of all. For even the Son of Man did not come to be served, but to serve, and to give his life as a ransom for many" (Mark 10:42-45).

D. E. Hoste, successor to renowned missionary Hudson Taylor as director of the China Inland Mission, was, through the booklet *If I Am to Lead*, one of my early mentors. In an excerpt taken from his biography, he describes spiritual leadership:

What is the essential difference between spurious and true Christian leadership? When a man, in virtue of an official position in the Church, demands the obedience of another, irrespective of the latter's reason and conscience, this is the spirit of tyranny.

When, on the other hand, by the exercise of tact and sympathy, by prayer, spiritual power and sound wisdom, one Christian worker is able to influence and enlighten another, so that the latter, through the medium of his own reason and conscience, is led to alter one course and adopt another, this is true spiritual leadership.[2]

These ideas helped shape my concept of leadership: as servanthood, and as the ability to influence, enlighten and motivate to change through the medium of one's reason and conscience.

Dwight Eisenhower is often lauded for his definition of leadership: getting someone else to do something that you want done because he wants to do it. John Perkins frequently echoes this idea. For some, this "getting" degenerates into a sinister kind of coercion. It can feel like King Louis's rant, as he sent his twin brother Philippe back to the dungeon and to the iron mask that hid his identity: "Wear it until you love it!"[3]

But Eisenhower understood servant leadership. Here is his full statement:

> Now I think, speaking roughly, by leadership we mean the art of getting someone else to do something that you want done because he wants to do it, not because your position of power can compel him to do it, or your position of authority. A commander of a regiment is not necessarily a leader. He has all of the appurtenances of power given by a set of Army regulations by which he can compel unified action. He can say to a body such as this, "Rise," and "Sit down." You do it exactly. But that is *not* leadership.[4] (emphasis added)

Leadership as the art of igniting internal motivations highlights the significance of identifying divine imprints. This idea was captured by a phrase of Walt Whitman: "I am the teacher of athletes, He that by me spreads a wider breast than my own proves the width of my own."[5]

I have never been an athletic coach, but I imagine that coaches view young athletes in this way: *I see potential in you. I make it my aim to maximize that potential. This will involve a measure of pain, but my purpose is to draw out of you your very best. You will, through my influence, become the athlete you were created to be.*

It eventually dawned on me that I too was a teacher of athletes. God had placed in my life young people created with potential and purpose. These youth were "emerging" leaders, for adolescents are most concerned about discovering who they are and why they exist. In a sense, the breadth of *my* leadership would become evident as they, through my influence, grew in *their* capacity to lead. My role was not to lead in the traditional sense, but rather to develop—through a transformative process—emerging leaders.

Emerging Leaders

Toward the end of my second decade in Denver, out of a desire to pass on leadership of the local work, I sought out a new director for the ministry. In the summer of '98, we hired someone I could groom to fill the director's position. The plan was for me to transition into functioning more as an ambassador and advisor.

Then I contracted leukemia.

The decade ended with me recovering from a bone marrow transplant and leaving the ministry in the hands of a novice. The battle with leukemia shook my world. I no longer had the entrepreneurial strength I had once possessed. Economic fears associated with the new millennium, followed by the 9/11 terrorist attacks, triggered major losses of donor support. Some called the office assuming I was dead!

I remember sharing feelings of disorientation with fellow board members of the Christian Community Development Association, figuring if anyone could empathize with my struggles, it would be these fellow urban ministry practitioners. I will never forget Bob Lupton's response:

> You got sick at a time you moved from being a young man to an old(er) man. You also got sick at a time your community changed.[6] You're like Rip van Winkle: you fell asleep a few years, woke up, and discovered everything has changed.

Things *had* changed. Neighborhood Ministries' director and other key staff had left. The organization was no longer guided by its core values. The high school group had been reshaped into an evangelistic program, where unruly youth played as they tolerated gospel messages. The whole operation was in disarray, led by adults with little understanding of evangelism *through* development.

I chose to reenter the ministry by directing the summer day camp—enlisting as my deputy a young woman named Raquel, whose family we had known since she was a child. (Shelly and I are godparents to her younger brother.) Raquel had served in various positions in the ministry since she was 16. With her help, I gathered a handful of high school students and designed a four-month process of preparing them to lead the summer day camp.

That summer, ministry leaders and parents visited and observed the camp. They marveled at the capacity and effectiveness of the youth leadership team. The relational dynamics between child and adolescent leader were different from anything any of us had ever observed. Potential and hope seemed to ignite within the children as they experienced being led by youth only a few years ahead of them in age. They could actually begin to envision leadership possibilities for their own lives.

By the end of the summer, the adult youth staff sought my help. The following year, we disbanded the high school club and replaced it with the Emerging Leaders Initiative—taking a crucial step toward a comprehensive philosophy of youth leadership development.

Notes

1. Fred Brown, "Gang fear lurks in shadows," in *Denver Post*, 7/15/2007, http://www.denverpost.com/brown/ci_6362438, accessed July 2015.
2. D. E. Hoste, *If I Am to Lead* (Singapore: OMF (IHQ) Ltd., 1987), p. 4.
3. *The Man in the Iron Mask* (United Artists, 1998), screenplay by Randall Wallace.
4. Dwight Eisenhower, Remarks at the Annual Conference of the Society for Personnel Administration, 5/12/54.
5. Walt Whitman, "Song of Myself," in *Leaves of Grass* (Mineola, NY: Dover Publications, Inc., 2007), p. 62.
6. Bob was referring to a phenomenon known as gentrification, which involves more affluent people moving into a low-income community, bringing with them resources and development, but often displacing poorer residents in the process.

Questions for Thought

1. Describe your beginnings. How did you get started in urban youth ministry?

2. What were some of the early lessons you learned from the youth you serve(d)?

3. When addressing groups of young people, do you sense that you are "scratching where they are itching"? Why or why not?

4. Are you a servant leader? Do you see yourself as a teacher of athletes? Why or why not?

5. What do you think of the apprentice approach to youth development? Are there places in your ministry where apprenticeship is (or could be) practiced?

Chapter 2

THE CHALLENGE

More young people are killed in Chicago than any other U.S. city. Since 2008, more than 530 youth have been killed in Chicago with nearly 80 percent of the homicides occurring in 22 African-American or Latino community areas on the city's South, Southwest and West sides.[1]

Through local newspapers and evening newscasts, the disturbing realities of youth violence reach suburban soccer moms, academy professors, rural farm families, and many others far removed from its direct influence. Branded into the American psyche is the media imagery of city streets swarming with ominous-looking youth wearing white muscle tees, sagging jeans and hoodies. It's hard to walk past anyone fitting that profile without feeling a foreboding sense of danger.

Even for those of us who were born, raised and live in the city, when we see a young person who fits the media stereotype, our response is akin to that of the climber who may love the mountains yet treads carefully in somber awareness of their dangers. For anyone who has grown up urban, threat-assessment is like a sixth sense, a way of life.

We call them at-risk youth. "At-risk" describes young people whose environment makes them most vulnerable to violence, abuse and delinquency. Considering the influence of modern media on social norms and values, even young people growing up in secure and healthy communities can be deemed, to some degree, "at-risk." But the setting most associated with the phrase is the inner city: those depressed urban sectors within major metropolitan areas where the population consists of the less educated and more impoverished, has a predominant minority presence (mostly African-American, Latino and Asian-American), and is characterized by a higher crime rate than other areas of the city.

These at-risk features of city life have a significant impact on youth ministry. "I don't know how to help him," a veteran youth leader cried. "He loves our basketball program. He's a good kid. But then he goes home, where gangsters and drug dealers surround him, always pressuring him to hang with them. He asks what God is doing, why He's allowing this. I honestly don't know how to respond."

Truth is, most youth leaders *don't* know how to respond. Never has the chasm between adults and youth been more pronounced. Experientially we cannot fathom the challenges of growing up urban today. Yes, we know statistics; we understand the dynamics of family and community brokenness. Yet such knowledge rarely translates into genuinely effective intervention and change. Too often those who speak directly to youth sound eerily like Job's counselors, spouting pious platitudes that sound right but have little to do with what's really going on.

Maybe, like the young man rioting in Baltimore, we are in need of an emphatic reminder (a "slap to the head") that we can do better.

Clouded by Assumptions

Years ago, I brought a group of kids back from a weekend mountain retreat in time to attend morning worship at a church in our neighborhood. The girls did not want to go in, because they had been taught that it was wrong to wear jeans in church.

I assured them that people would understand and would even be excited about their presence. I was wrong—terribly wrong—and was sorely chastised for my "transgression."

You may laugh; dress codes have indeed relaxed over the years. But the disconnect is still there; it just shows up in different ways. Many a youth leader has said, "I want to take the ministry in this new direction; I know it is the right thing to do. But the leadership won't allow for it. It doesn't fit with their expectations; *there's too much pressure to keep things the same.*"

A significant reason why self-examination is not something people who work with urban youth do well is context. Most youth programs are part of something bigger: a church or parachurch organization. A governing body's expectations wield a great deal of control; their presence can bring any innovation or new ideas to a grinding halt.

Behind a controlling body's expectations lies a deeper problem: prevailing assumptions. "Give them healthy activities, lots of love and the gospel; God will take care of the rest," I have often heard adults assert. "The cream [i.e., youth destined for success] always rises to the top." "I survived my adolescent years; so will they."

There is a measure of truth to this kind of thinking. But, as the messages coming out of the hip-hop and rap music genre reveal, today's young people are experiencing an anguish of soul and a confusion about life that are tearing them apart. Sitting back and letting things happen has become an untenable response. Youth are struggling, and that struggle is affecting families and communities. It is tearing at the very fabric of society.

Enter the youth leader. They are special—a unique breed. Possessing great passion for Christ, their earnest desire is that young people come to know Christ and grow in Him. While there are some who treat youth ministry as a ladder toward something greater, most pursue their mission with abundant zeal and at times a reckless abandon. Often I have heard youth leaders cry out: "Satan never rests and neither should we!" (Which inevitably evokes my response: "Satan was never meant to be your role model. God is your role model, and He rested on the seventh day!")

The fact of the matter is, misplaced zeal can be damaging. Most youth workers burn out after two or three years. This is hardly a surprise; inner-city ministry is demanding work! But faulty assumptions—the underlying beliefs upon which actions are based—can speed the process of wearing leaders down, especially when those beliefs do not fit reality.

In their masterful work *Divided by Faith*, Christian Smith and Michael Emerson identified some commonly held assumptions within the evangelical worldview that have produced behaviors inconsistent with belief. (In the case they were studying, the primary disconnect between belief and practice involved affirming reconciliation while practicing racial isolation.) In a similar way, most approaches to serving at-risk youth are rooted in commonly held assumptions. Here are a few of them:

- Evangelism is the primary task of the church, and therefore the primary focus of youth ministry.
- Christian maturity is measured by one's knowledge of Scripture.
- Leaders, like cream, rise to the top. Therefore the youth leader's task is to lead youth to Christ and disciple them, giving special attention to the best and brightest.
- Adolescents lack the maturity to lead. Especially those within the at-risk youth population—handicapped by such social deficits as poverty, single parenting, poor education, gang presence and the like, they need people who first and foremost love and encourage them. Leadership development is nice but not necessary.
- Developing leadership capacity in youth is a transactional process. Leadership growth happens when youth are proficient in carrying out assigned tasks with a positive attitude.

Most assumptions are based in truth but have just enough error mixed in to steer us in wrong directions. This makes them faulty, and acting on faulty assumptions leads to great frustrations.

Understanding Community, Mission and Adolescents

It will take conclusions more aligned with truth and reality to make a difference in the areas of community, mission and adolescents.

1. The Ministry Context

Urban ministry and community development pioneer John Perkins says, "Two things in society are broken: the family and the community." The reality is that youth are byproducts of that brokenness. Youth are individuals, to be sure, with the power to effect outcomes by their own choices. But they have been influenced, shaped, and to greater and lesser degrees, controlled by their socioeconomic environment. They have been touched by brokenness; they must navigate and interpret life through the grid of family and/or community dysfunction.

Reaching these youth requires more than an understanding of the city and empathy for its young residents. It requires the ability to translate the gospel message into their context—to become a conduit through which Jesus addresses their deepest needs.

I remember experiencing a feeling of helplessness as kids dropped out of school, engaged in acts of violence, and experienced the stresses brought on by poverty and family instability—all the while telling them, "Jesus loves you." The Jesus I spoke of early in my ministry had little to say about young people's social needs. It took a rereading of the Gospels and meeting John Perkins to realize that preaching the gospel includes a profound social engagement.

The Scriptures describe Jesus as "a man of sorrows, and acquainted with grief" (Isaiah 53:3, *KJV*). Yet I've observed presentations in which youth *never* pick up on the idea that Jesus is acquainted with *their* grief.

Contextualization is more than an academic exercise. It's a physical one as well. It's not just about what is spoken. It's about where and how we live.

When I began working with inner-city youth, I lived in the suburbs of Denver, near the seminary I attended. After two years, I moved into the city—into the same community where the young people I had been working with lived. The first week I was there, my house was broken into—twice.

I remember trembling and staring in fear at the broken window in my living room. Then some of the neighborhood kids came over. You know what their response was? They looked, nodded their heads and said, "Now you understand. You're one of us now." My life and message had gained a context. I could now say that Jesus was acquainted with their grief, and do so with credibility.

This does not require experiencing all the same traumas they do (although it was helpful that the problem of theft in the community became *my* problem, and that motivated me to join other neighbors in working to solve it). But context matters. Positioning matters.

The Bible tells us, "The Word became flesh and made his dwelling among us" (John 1:14). The axiom rings as true for the city minister as it does for the foreign missionary: To the best of your ability, you live among the people you serve.

2. The Nature of the Task

Most youth leaders see their primary mission as leading kids into a personal relationship with Jesus Christ. This mission, vital as it is, becomes compromised and even polluted when it is pursued outside the Kingdom context of loving God and people.

I will never forget when I first heard inner-city mission leader Bob Lupton talk about a "theology of neighbor." Immediately a red flag went up: *I'm a Christian, and I've never heard of a "theology of neighbor."* My first reaction was suspicion. Then I thought, *Wait a minute. God's greatest command is to love Him and love my neighbor. Having a theology of neighbor makes sense.* What followed was horror: *Why* don't *I have a theology of neighbor? Why would a theology concerning God's greatest command make me suspicious? What's wrong with me?*

I have dear friends—wonderful Christian leaders—who struggle with treating the Great Command as the *greatest* command. The best they can do is put loving God and neighbor *on par* with preaching the gospel. There are strong socioeconomic drivers behind this that we will examine later.

Allowing the Great Commission (which most view as evangelism apart from disciple making) to override the Great Command (loving God and neighbor) creates a perspective that reduces people to "souls" in need of saving, and turns compassion into an evangelistic technique. What does treating the Great Command as the greatest command look like? Loving neighbor becomes the context in which good news is shared. Think of it this way: Before the meal can be served (preaching), guests must be properly greeted (loved) and the table set. The youth leader's first order of business becomes loving kids and creating a ministry setting that is conducive to discovery and growth.

3. The Adolescent Experience

Then there is the young person himself or herself. Who are these strange creatures? Everyone must journey through adolescence to reach adulthood. Adults know this, although we do not like to think about it very much. Generally we're thankful to have survived the journey, and we tend to view youth ministry as helping youth make it through this life stage with a minimal amount of pain and damage.

For youth growing up urban, a dynamic interplay of developmental forces is at work. Inwardly, there are the physiological and psychological changes inherent within normal adolescent development. Adolescence is generally understood as that prolonged developmental bridge between childhood and adulthood, generally including the teenage years and early twenties. It is a uniquely turbulent phase of life, often filled with what G. Stanley Hall, the father of modern adolescent psychology, called "sturm und drang" (storm and stress) as emerging adults wrestle with matters of self-identity, capacity, belief and direction.

All youth take this developmental journey, but those at risk do so through a particular sociocultural grid: the inner city, where formative adolescent development strains against such negative forces as poverty, family brokenness, and a culture of violence.

Realities such as these—compounded by media images that paint urban youth as out of control and dangerous—can mesmerize and overwhelm those trying to make a difference in a child's life. But they also can mislead. It is like watching a magician skilled in the art of deception: Our attention becomes riveted in one direction, when the answers we seek lie somewhere else. We can become so fixed on the pain and agony of the city that we miss the implications of basic adolescent development.

Consider this. If adolescence is a normal stage in human development, and therefore by God's design, it should raise questions: Where is God in all this? What is the church's responsibility to young people during the formative years of their lives? If adolescence is a God-thing, in what ways should the reality of that experience shape and influence youth ministry engagement? Such questions should be asked not only by youth leaders but also by all who are concerned about transformative urban youth development.

Not a Time to Hinder

In Mark 10, Jesus responds to an episode involving children with an important lesson on discipleship. This brief story deserves careful scrutiny:

People were bringing little children to Jesus for him to place his hands on them, but the disciples rebuked them. When Jesus saw this, he was indignant. He said to them, "Let the little children come to me, and do not hinder them, for the kingdom of God belongs to such as these. Truly I tell you, anyone who will not receive the kingdom of God like a little child will never enter it." And he took the children in his arms, placed his hands on them and blessed them (vv. 13-16).

In Jesus' day, it was a common practice for parents to bring their children to great leaders to be blessed by them. Why the disciples rebuked the parents is unclear; perhaps they discerned that Jesus was weary, or felt that He should be spared the bother of children. The teaching that emerged from the encounter was clear: To enter the Kingdom, one must receive "like a little child"—that is, as a child receives, with receptivity and dependence. These qualities are necessary for discipleship.

But is that the sole takeaway from this passage? Are we merely to learn that adults need to be receptive, like children? Or was there more to what Jesus was saying?

Mark's Gospel reveals a heightened sensitivity to Jesus' humanity. His is the only account that describes Jesus' emotions so vividly. Jesus, Mark recounts, was *indignant* over the disciples' choice to turn away children. Being indignant is "feeling or showing anger because of something unjust or unworthy."[2] This is significant. To Jesus, the disciples were not committing a simple error. They were attempting to do something unjust. Their actions evoked righteous anger!

What made Him so angry? It's hard to imagine that Jesus was angry because an object lesson was being thwarted. A much more reasonable interpretation is that there was something terribly wrong with impeding children's access to Him.

Jesus' righteous anger led Him to issue two commands—or rather, one command reinforced by its negative counterpart. The first was: "Permit!" To permit is to let in or allow access. Adults must allow children access to Jesus. He then reinforced this pos- itive instruction with a negative: "Do not hinder!" Under no cir- cumstances should children be hindered, impeded or obstructed from coming to Jesus.

To treat this as an admonition for parents to bring children to be blessed by Jesus, as if it were simply a call for baby dedications, misses the bigger picture. Absent Jesus' intervention, the disciples could have easily diverted the children away from Him. The par- ents could have kept them away in the first place. Children may be receptive, but adults control access. When the disciples hindered the access of children to Jesus, it became an abuse of power. Jesus sized it up immediately and cried, "Unjust!"

Fast forward to today. Now, as then, adults set the agenda for youth ministry. We hold the power. Adults—pastors, youth lead- ers, ministry directors, parents—exercise a great amount of control over if, when and how children have access to Jesus.

What would Jesus say about how we use this power?

- Would Jesus view the assumptions that guide most youth ministries as honest, well-intended mistakes? Or would they make Him angry?
- What would unhindered access to Jesus look like? Would it consist of more than a "Bless you!" and a hug? Would there be opportunity for, as Francis Schaeffer described it, honest answers to honest questions? Would attention be given to guidance? Would access involve a process of discovering who God really is, and who young people are in relation to Him? And what about leaders? Would there be greater transparency in leadership? Greater openness? Would leaders be committed to living lives worth imitat- ing (see 1 Corinthians 11:1)?
- Finally, how important is this? Could the absence of a transformative ministry presence be a contributing fac- tor in the growing youth violence in our cities? Is this

hindering of young people's access to all Jesus has to offer them important enough to evoke anger? Is youth ministry a justice issue? I believe it is.

Youth are our future. Yet we do not seem to know what to do with them.

It was Einstein who said, "You cannot solve problems with the same level of thinking you used when you created them."

No single youth leader (or church or denomination or parachurch ministry) can be blamed for the growing unrest among urban youth today. A quick review of the state of societies around the globe provides plenty of directions in which blame can be cast.

But when it comes to *responsibility*—being able, compelled and obligated to respond—Jesus says that's on us, the people of God. The time has come to weave what I call transformational discipleship into the fabric of urban youth ministry.

Time to Reconnect

Winston Churchill once said, "Criticism is easy. Achievement is more difficult."

Moving urban ministry past lament and excuses to genuine achievement requires stepping away from the complexities of ministry in the urban jungle, just for a moment, to take a fresh look at the fundamental youth ministry task.

1. First, we must do something that may seem elementary but is extremely important: We must *rethink the purpose of youth ministry*. With humility, we must look again at the basic questions: Who are these enigmatic young people? What are their felt needs? What is the church's responsibility to children and youth during these formative years of life?

2. Then we must *revisit our theology*. What is the mission of the church? What does it mean to be created in the image of God? How do these and other theological truths, such as those embedded in the Great Command and Great Commission, impact youth ministry? What did Jesus mean when He said, "Permit the children to come to me"? What does it mean to "be transformed by the renewing of your mind" (Romans 12:2)?

3. Finally, we must engage in the hard but necessary work of *pressing purpose and theology into clear plans of action*. Form must follow function. Youth leaders are *leaders*, and the first task of leadership is to define reality. This means designing a ministry structure and process that reflect (with integrity and cohesion) core beliefs and objectives.

Time for New Ideas

I believe youth ministries are *called* and (thanks to the presence of local churches) strategically *positioned* to make an impact on youth development in the city centers of our world. I believe such influence is critical to stemming the growing tide of dysfunction and unrest within the modern-day youth population. But this will require significant changes in the way youth ministry is currently perceived, as well as substantive adjustments to how youth ministry is carried out. It is time for an infusion of new ideas. Some such ideas are captured in the phrase "transformational discipleship."

- Transformational discipleship is the outgrowth of a theological construct. I have spent my ministry life pursuing the question, *How can the church animate (bring to life) leadership capacity among youth native to high-risk communities?* To answer this question, I have found myself examining truths related to mission, growing up urban, the image of God, and leadership. Then I connected the dots ("If A, B, C, and D, then what?") and pressed them into a philosophy and strategic approach.

- Transformational discipleship speaks to the essence of youth ministry, not youth ministry as a whole. There are many wonderfully creative ministries serving the needs of urban youth. Transformational discipleship does not diminish the need for specialized programs, such as sports, music, art, literacy, drama, advocacy, dance, and others. Specialized ministries of all kinds are important and sorely needed.

- The purpose of transformational discipleship is not to replace such ministries, but to enrich them by placing transforming young minds and growing through leading at the center of urban ministry activity.

The primary objective of this book is to unpack this ministry concept. The first section presents the need for such an approach, the history behind its development, and a working definition. The second section establishes a foundational paradigm that is theological (the biblical premises behind the concept) and ethnographical (the social, cultural and economic context in which youth ministry is carried out). The final section addresses how to build a transformational discipleship ministry culture and infuse the concept into new and existing youth ministry programs.

Notes

1. Kari Lydersen and Carlos Javier Ortiz, "Chicago Reporter: More young people are killed in Chicago than any other American City" (Chicago, IL: The Black Star Project, January 31, 2012).

2. "Indignant" at www.merriam-webster.com, accessed July 2015.

Questions for Thought

1. In what ways are youth at risk in your neighborhood (or another community God has given you a heart for)? In what ways does the environment make them vulnerable to abuse, neglect and delinquency?

2. What are some of the assumptions upon which you have built, or plan to build, your youth ministry? How solid are those assumptions?

3. Which characterizes your ministry more, evangelism or loving God and neighbor? How might making loving neighbor the context in which the good news of the gospel is shared change your ministry?

4. In what ways does your ministry permit youth to come to Jesus? Are there ways in which your ministry may be hindering youth from coming to Jesus?

Chapter 3

MY JOURNEY

Life is a Story. Stories matter.

I t was Sunday, October 27. Shortly after 12 noon. Vienna, Austria, time.

I was a student at the Vienna Conservatory. While completing the instrumental requirements for a double major—music education instrumental and music education vocal—at Fredonia State University College in New York, I had learned that the music conservatory in Vienna would be a great place to study voice. Plus it would look good on my résumé.

About 10 students from our college attended the conservatory that year. One in particular triggered my "inner rogue"; I was friendly but with ulterior motives in mind. Things were going well, I thought, until she disclosed that she was a Christian.

Disgust quickly turned to anger. At that point in my life, I had little respect for Christians, having encountered many who seemed hypocritical in their words and behaviors. (Of course, like many resisters to faith, I saw only what I wanted to see.) I classified them as "airheads."

But still, I was curious. My path to Vienna had differed slightly from that of my classmates. I had toured Romania with a school choir for three weeks that summer. At the end of the tour, the choir flew back to the States, but I stayed and traveled through Europe. I took a train from Bucharest, Romania, through Bulgaria to Athens,

Greece. Then I traveled by boat to the boot of Italy, from which point I hitchhiked and rode more trains along the eastern coast to Venice, and then on to Vienna, Austria.

The boat trip included a stop at the island of Corfu. This was a rustic paradise: For three days, I slept under the stars, gazed at the hypnotic blue waters of the Mediterranean Sea, and pondered my life. I remember staring at a cross, wondering if it might be time to revisit "that Christian thing."

Perhaps that is why, after grumbling a bit, I asked the girl who had become the object of my disgust where she went to church while in Vienna. She said she attended an International Chapel. "International Chapel?" I said. "I've never been to one of those before." And then, not waiting for an actual invitation, I added, "I think I'll go."

Sunday came, and I arrived early. This "chapel" did not meet in a traditional church building, but rather in what looked like the back of an old theatre. People were mingling prior to the Sunday School hour.

In addition to its unorthodox meeting place, the church was peculiar in two ways. The first was the people. This was an English-speaking church in the heart of a German-speaking city. Some of the attenders were folks like me: college students from universities around the world. There were also diplomats with their families. As the gateway to the Eastern Bloc countries, Vienna was a base city for missionaries serving the persecuted church in Eastern Europe, so there were also people in various stages of coming and going from numerous locations in that region.

These groups converged into what appeared to be a strange mixture of people. As they mingled, I overheard different languages: some English over here, some German over there, something that sounded Slovakian in yet another group. It was the most diverse crowd I had ever encountered. What was most striking was the way they related to each other. They seemed at ease in their diversity, unforced, conveying a natural camaraderie with one another.

The second peculiarity was the Sunday School teacher. He was a handsome, middle-aged man, physically fit, with a smile that, again, put people at ease. He stood while he taught, Bible in hand. I knew the Bible well enough to recognize the quotations laced throughout his talk. What was puzzling was that he never opened the book. He didn't have to. His relationship to the Scriptures seemed more like that of an old friend than an interpreter or expositor. I could not separate the words from his life. His faith did not seem forced in any way; it simply was. As I watched and listened, I thought: *This guy, these people—they're not fitting my "airhead" definition of Christians!*

I left church confused. The next day I ran into the girl. "So what did you think?" she asked. I told her it had left me confused. She handed me a small Bible—the New Testament and Psalms—and departed.

I took that Bible back to my dorm and had a conversation with a God I wasn't sure existed. It went something like this:

> God, they say You are real and this book is true. Well, I have criticized Christians, put them down, and even done cruel things to people because they were Christians. But there's one thing I've never done: I've never read the book for myself. So here's the deal: I'm going to read this book, and I'm going to read it good. If it's true, then I'm Yours. If it's not true, I'll never again consider Christianity to be a valid option for my life.

I spent the next two weeks reading that Bible. At first I expected discrepancies and fallacies to jump out at me. But none did. Instead, I found myself increasingly captivated by this person named Jesus. The more I read about Him, the more I wanted to know Him.

Two weeks later, on October 27, I returned to that church. Again the people were impressive in the way they loved one another. And once again I was amazed by the genuineness of the Sunday School teacher.

This time, though, it was the preacher who sealed the deal. I don't remember anything else he said, but at one point he held up his Bible and declared: "I'm not preaching . . ." and rattled off a list of denominational names. "I'm not preaching the Baptist religion or the Catholic religion. . . I'm preaching Jesus Christ as He is revealed in this book!"

I had never heard anyone play down their denomination and lift up Jesus Christ. *"This is it,"* I said to myself. *"Jesus is for real!"* I was excited, so much so that I thought I must be a Christian!

As soon as the service ended, I rushed over to the Sunday School teacher. "Bud! Bud! I think I'm a Christian!"

"Are you sure?" he asked.

"No!" I shouted.

He sat me down and shared this verse:

And this is the testimony: God has given us eternal life, and this life is in his Son. Whoever has the Son has life; whoever does not have the Son of God does not have life. I write these things to you who believe in the name of the Son of God so that you may know that you have eternal life (1 John 5:11-13).

Bud said, "You pray, and then I'll pray."

I closed my eyes. The first thing out of my mouth was: "God, I'm a sinner." I don't know why I said that. It must have come from my reading of the Bible. But I said it and knew what it meant. "God, I'm a sinner. I've been living life on my own terms and in my own way. Thank You, Jesus, for dying for my sins. Please take my life now; make it what You want it to be."

That was it. Bud said, "Amen," and we opened our eyes.

Bud's smile quickly turned to laughter. He looked me in the eyes and said, "Ted, as a brother in Christ, I love you. If there's anything I can do for you, you let me know."

He introduced me to his wife. She greeted me warmly, shaking my hand. She glanced at her husband, who was still smiling broadly. Still shaking my hand, she glanced at him a second time, and a third. Then, realizing what had happened, she threw her arms around me. She was crying! "Just wait," she said. "You'll see, you'll see."

Me? I was happy to have made a decision. I walked through the crowd, shaking people's hands. "I'm a Christian now. Isn't that wonderful?" I spent the afternoon with my newfound Christian friends.

I did not really fathom what had happened until that night. I was lying in bed, thinking about the day's events, when I sensed that something was different. How to describe it? It was as if I had been studying for a long time, building a natural tension I did not know was there, until someone snuck up from behind and gave me a back rub—"Ooh, I didn't realize I was so tense!"

In a much more profound way than that, the tension, the anxiety, the fears and the turmoil—those things that had been a natural part of my non-Christian life—faded away. I had not been aware that they were there until that moment, when I realized they were gone. That's when I knew with certainty that God had entered my life and was already making changes from the inside out.

I began talking to a God I now knew existed, baring my soul with an openness and freedom I had never thought possible. My first words were about my dad: how I missed him, how growing up without him had been such a struggle. "This is a void in my life, Lord, but it's one You're going to fill," I said tearfully. "In fact, You're going to fill all the voids in my life, because You are my heavenly Father."

Days later I read: "A father to the fatherless, a defender of widows, is God in his holy dwelling" (Psalm 68:5).

Anywhere but There!

My new faith opened a new perspective on life. My aspirations shifted from leading a high school music department to entering full-time missionary service. With great zeal I prayed: "God, I will go anywhere in the world You want me to go, *except the kind of place I grew up in.*" I could not fathom going back to the old neighborhood. Surely God would deem such a caveat inconsequential in light of my eagerness to follow Him anywhere (except there) in the world!

Perhaps a bit of context would be helpful here. Bellport is a small town located 60 miles east of New York City. Nestled on Long Island's south shore, its colonial-style architecture and laid-back pace made it an almost idyllic place to live. Middle- to upper-class families enjoyed the pleasant experience of calling it home.

But like many of the coastal towns along the southern strip of Long Island, the railroad ran right through Bellport. And for those who lived on the north side of them, those tracks divided more than the town's geography. They became a metaphor for a far deeper divide between black and white, rich and poor.

I was six years old when we moved into North Bellport. My younger sister (the historian of the family) believes we were the first African Americans to move into this newly formed hamlet. Demographics changed rapidly: Within five short years, the community became predominantly black, with some Puerto Ricans and Caucasians.

In many ways, my childhood was a happy experience. Food was cheap and bountiful: Cheerios or fried eggs for breakfast; peanut butter and mayonnaise sandwiches for lunch; ham hock stew, creamed tuna over bread, or fried chicken necks at dinner—I have many fond memories of food (my mother fed me steak at six months!). Who could forget the Sunday after-church family visits to the Ponderosa and its all-you-can-eat buffet!

I have fond people memories as well: Saturday family outings at Heckscher State Park; visits to my cousins (one family, 10 kids) in Glen Cove; and playing games with other children in the neighborhood. Favorites were Running Bases (a friend and I played catch near "bases"—large rocks or wooden planks—as other kids tried to run the bases without getting tagged), Marbles (our dirt driveway was perfect for carving out terrain), and Bottle Caps (this was the granddaddy of them all! We'd use drywall ripped from a nearby abandoned house to draw a game board with numbered squares on the street pavement. Then we'd find used bottle caps, scrape them on the ground until they were smooth and shiny, and compete to see who'd be the first to run the board by flicking the caps in and out of the squares).

Life changed dramatically in the seventh grade. I left the safety and familiarity of elementary school for the uncertain world of middle school. Adjusting to a new environment made my middle-school experience uncomfortable. The presence of gangs made it dangerous.

I remember being confronted one time in the hallway by a group from my neighborhood:

"Hey Ted, you gonna join our gang?" they asked ominously.

"No," I replied. "I've already joined the music department." Before they could process my response, I scurried off to the music room!

The music department became a safe haven in a hostile world. During free periods, and often also during the short breaks between classes, I was there: singing, practicing my trombone or just hanging out. I became a music nerd, with musicians as my closest friends, to the exclusion of almost everyone else.

That pattern continued in high school, where I emerged as a leader in the music department. There were times, walking through the halls, when I would hear shouts of "Nigger" and "Uncle Tom" in the same day! I ignored them. Music was my life; my goal was to graduate college and direct a high school music department.

When the time came to leave for college, the message was loud and clear: "You're leaving North Bellport. You made it. Don't come back." To me, the caveat in my prayer—I will go anywhere in the world *except*. . . —made perfect sense.

The Identity Button

After my conversion experience in Vienna, Pastor Mathews quickly became my mentor and confidant. We met on Tuesday mornings at his apartment, located on the edge of the city at the foot of the Vienna Woods. We walked those woods often. He was a wonderful listener; I shared my thoughts and concerns, and also asked a multitude of questions. He always responded with wise, loving counsel.

But in the second year, he picked up on my caveat. Over time, his gentle probing turned into a direct challenge: "Ted, you should consider serving in the inner city. City ministry could use someone like you."

My response was irrational yet consistent: "I just can't go back [to an inner-city environment]."

One fateful Tuesday morning, my pastor again brought up the possibility of my serving God in the inner city. Again I resisted. As I stood at the front door, saying my goodbyes, I noticed a puzzled look on his face.

"What is it?" I asked.

"I'm just wondering," he replied, "if you realize you are black?"

I immediately broke down. Pastor Mathews rushed me to his living room, trying frantically to console me. At first what spewed out of me seemed to be raw emotion, irrational and unintelligible. It was clear that a great conflict had been bottled up for a long time, and now it was pouring out of me.

In his probing, Pastor Mathews had pushed my identity button, unleashing a flood of unresolved questions. Who was I? Nigger? Uncle Tom? An African American with an operatic voice, a black musician who was lousy at improvisation but could sight-read atonal music—what kind of anomaly was that? "Definitions" coming out of the Black Power movement had horrified me. I did not want to "shuffle," I preferred Standard English to Ebonics, and ethnic differences fascinated me.

Over the years, such discrepancies had caused some of my hue to question my "blackness." Secretly I sometimes questioned it as well.

I had an identity problem. Questions, and the shame and guilt that accompanied them, had remained bottled up inside, until Pastor Mathews pushed the button and unleashed the flood.

As the initial wave of emotion subsided, a new reality came into focus: To truly serve God, I could run from this no longer, because God made me in His image, and He made me black. I had not linked the image of God to personal identity before, but at that moment I realized that only the former could bring true meaning to the latter.

Eventually I calmed down and declared in prayer an openness to serving God *anywhere*. "God, if You want me to go to the inner city, I will."

A Gift Named John Peyton

Anxious to begin the next chapter of my life, I dropped the double major, graduated college with a B.A. Degree in Music, and enrolled in Denver Theological Seminary. Not that I had any intention of graduating from seminary; I simply thought it would be a good place to learn a few things about "American" Christianity. I still had my sights set on ministry overseas.

That is, until I met John Peyton.

Against the backdrop of a predominantly white school, John Peyton stood out as larger than life. He was a tall, lean, dark-skinned African American. He was charismatic; he could be loud at times, but even when silent his presence would fill a room. His testimony was similar to that of another dynamic Christian leader: Tom Skinner. For Skinner, it was from the jaws of the Harlem Lords street gang that God had rescued him from certain death; for John, it was from the clutches of the Black Panther Party.

I remember being introduced to John in the student center. I watched as he sized me up and, predictably, found me wanting. He mumbled something dismissive, like "You just another educated white n---." I sized him up as well: He was a gift. This man of similar hue but different background; this gritty, dynamic leader within the black community; this man of strong convictions and deep devotion to Christ—he didn't know it yet, but we were about to become good friends.

As I had done with Bud and Pastor Mathews, I "hung on to his coat sleeves." I followed John around, meeting with him whenever I could. At first we argued, challenging more the caricatures we had of each other than the real people. Gradually argument gave way to great, substantive discussions.

"If you're black, you belong in the city," he would assert.

"Blackness does not bind me to the city," I retorted. "We as a people are bigger than that. God may lead me to the city, but I don't *have* to be there."

From divergent points of view, we tackled the issues of our day: race, culture, the black church, white people, and how we might make a difference in our world. Often we'd go to his house in the suburbs and debate while devouring a pot of chit'lins. (Chitterlings have a strong, distinct smell. They repel most people, but for chit'lin lovers like John and me, they are mouth-watering. One day while visiting in his home, we heard a knock. Standing at the door was a black man. He held out an empty bowl. "I smell wrinkle steak!" he cried. Of course we had to share.)

As we talked, our admiration for each other grew. As the time came for him to graduate and move on, he shared something I have always cherished: "Ted, I think we are ahead of our time."

John went on to lead a large multi-ethnic church in Virginia. Shortly after John left seminary, I began working with youth in Denver, first as a Sunday School teacher at a storefront mission, and later on staff with Youth for Christ. It was strange: I had won the argument, but lost the war. The more I argued that I did not have to go to the city, the more I was drawn there. John's perspective had enriched my own, and in the process changed my life and the entire course of my ministry.

Questions for Thought

1. Are there caveats to your willingness to serve God anywhere He may call you to go? What might your next step be in opening your heart to challenging things God may want you to do for His Kingdom?

2. Do you struggle with questions about your own ethnic identity or other aspects of how God has made you? Have you considered whether these struggles may be hindering you from saying an unequivocal yes to God's call on your life?

3. Is there someone in your life who comes at things from a completely different perspective than your own? Do you try to avoid this person and the disagreements you have with him or her, or do you embrace the opportunity to exchange ideas and learn from each other?

Chapter 4

TAPESTRY

Your eyes saw my unformed body;
all the days ordained for me were written in your book
before one of them came to be.

PSALM 139:16

There I was, a doctoral student, beginning the day as I did each day during the two-week block of classes at Bakke University in Seattle: reading and sipping coffee at Starbucks.

This particular morning I was distracted. The day before, Professor Ray Bakke had taken the class to his home, affectionately known as Bakken, where we walked a path through his backyard forest. It was a *Via Dolorosa*-type experience. (The *Via Dolorosa* is the road in Jerusalem that Jesus walked to His crucifixion; today it is marked by "stations" representing significant moments along that journey to the cross.) We paused at markers along the way, reading and reflecting upon stories from key events in Christian history.

In one of his lectures, Dr. Bakke drew two intersecting lines, one horizontal and one vertical, to illustrate different perspectives on God. The vertical line, dominant among Christians in the West, envisions God as one who values expedience: "Win the world for Christ in this generation!" Christians within Eastern orthodox cultures, however, embrace a more horizontal perspective. They envision a God who above all else values faithfulness: "Stay true to the end of time."

As a Western Christian, my relationship with God leaned vertical. I focused on God's direct dealings with me. Dr. Bakke had introduced a missing, or at best weak, dimension of my spiritual life. Yes, God loves me directly, but He also loves me *eternally*. In this sense, He is vast, mysterious, a God who "hovers" (see Genesis 1:2) over my life, and who "in all things works for the good" (see Romans 8:28). This horizontal perspective was new to me.

Pondering the horizontal perspective began to disturb me. That morning, right there in the middle of the coffee shop, it erupted into a Damascus Road-type encounter with God. First I trembled. Then I heard (or thought I heard) a clear, audible voice: "You are Theodore Roosevelt Travis III, son of Theodore Roosevelt Travis Jr. and grandson of Abraham Lincoln Mack!"

I began to fathom—almost *feel*—the movement of God in my family history. "Poppa," my grandfather, a Methodist preacher and son of a white employer and black maid, became the patriarch of a large family. When I was a child, he would take me in his arms and say, "This here is my preacher boy!" My father, a bricklayer by trade, died when I was 15 years old from cancer and a bleeding ulcer—a slow and deteriorating death. Yet, a few years before his passing, he underwent a transformation I did not understand until shortly after the same thing happened to me: He became a Christian.

On that day in Seattle, I heard God say, "Stop. Remember. You are the son and grandson of these men. This is your lineage. I am the Lord." These words shook me to my core.

The dictionary defines missiology as the study of Christian missions, their methods and purposes.[1] Missiology is the study of God's workings through time. It is about connecting the dots of life in order to grasp divine meanings.

Many view their family history with a sense of pride, but not all recognize or appreciate God's hand in it. Apparently neither had I, until that moment. Suddenly Jesus' words in John 5:17 ("My Father is always at his work to this very day, and I too am working"), and those of the psalmist ("Lord, you have been our dwelling place throughout all generations" [Psalm 90:1]) erupted with new meaning.

Decades into my journey with Jesus, I can now appreciate more deeply those life-changing events—both during and before my own sojourn on Earth—that have shaped me and my transformational discipleship ministry approach.

Lessons from the Journey

In his devotional classic *A Diary of Private Prayer*, Scottish theologian John Baillie ended a day with this reflection:

> Almighty God, in this hour of quiet I seek communion with thee.... All day long I have toiled and striven; but now, in stillness of heart and in the clear light of eternity, *I would ponder the pattern my life has been weaving.*[2] (emphasis added)

Life weaves a pattern. It tells a story. Reflecting on our personal journeys reveals much about who we are and why we do what we do. I had never really appreciated that until my experience in Seattle. Once I began to consider this perspective, I could clearly see lessons contributing to transformational discipleship that began a long time ago.

A Divine Conspiracy

> But do not forget this one thing, dear friends: With the Lord a day is like a thousand years, and a thousand years are like a day. The Lord is not slow in keeping his promise, as some understand slowness. Instead he is patient with you, not wanting anyone to perish, but everyone to come to repentance (2 Peter 3:8-9).

It still astounds me that 40 years ago, God's desire that all "come to repentance" culminated for me, on an October Sunday in Vienna, in my salvation. Truly a life-changing moment! Yet over time I have realized that this event was part of a much larger conspiracy.

When it began I cannot say. But in hindsight I find God to be as crafty as He is patient. Life in North Bellport, a father's death, an identity crisis, a decision to study overseas, pondering life on Corfu, meeting a Christian girl, inviting myself to an international chapel—I cannot prove it, but I sense that these events were all pieces of a larger tapestry. They were not as random as they first appeared. Somehow God orchestrated this. He set me up!

Talk about conspiracy! I later discovered that when that Christian girl saw my interest in Christianity, she alerted Pastor Mathews. He, in turn, mailed a letter to a group he called "Serious Ones," telling them about me and asking them to pray. Unbeknownst to me, when I asked Jesus into my heart that Sunday, there were strangers back in the States praying, in solidarity with God's expressed desire, on my behalf!

It was a divine conspiracy. I never had a chance. For that, I am profoundly grateful.

You have a story. We all do. We all have unique threads to contribute to the tapestry God is weaving; we are all a part of the divine conspiracy.

When I first moved into Five Points to work with kids, I knew I was returning to the kind of place I had once escaped. Although the neighborhood was located in a different city, it had all the elements I had long feared. The youth I would meet there experienced challenges very similar to those I had faced as a teenager in my neighborhood.

But one thing was different. I knew something they did not know—something that gave me a strategic edge. I knew that God was either *in* them or *on* them—either He resided in them, because they had given their lives to Christ, or He was influencing them, using people and circumstances to draw their attention to Himself.

To be sure, youth ministry engages in evangelism and advocacy and relief. But all those things happen within a much bigger context. When you enter youth ministry or otherwise get involved in the lives of youth, you become part of a divine conspiracy. You are now part of a young person's story and God's agenda within that story. It is important to see our interactions with the youth we love and serve from this perspective.

Image Matters

> So God created mankind in his own image, in the image of God he created them; male and female he created them (Genesis 1:27).

In 1990, tennis star Andre Agassi was part of an ad campaign promoting Canon's EOS Rebel camera. In the ad he famously declared: "Image is everything."

He (or the advertising company, anyway) was right. Those three words struck a chord with viewers, making the campaign one of the most successful in the history of modern-day advertising. Image, as an expression of identity, is "everything."

Why is image everything? Because God made it everything. "So God created mankind in his own image." Every living, breathing person is an image bearer—of God!

When, during my racial identity crisis, I said, "God made me in His image, and He made me black. . . . I need to find out what that means," I had instinctively linked together two powerful definers of self: the image of God and self-identity. In the camera commercials, Agassi presented image as an *impression*—the persona one shows to the world. But image is more than that.

Image is a *reflection*—it mirrors its source. There is only one   ❦ image that truly matters, and that is the image of God. That image reveals itself in a blend of characteristics unique to every person—a combination of traits that shapes identity. Things like race and culture are part of the identity equation, but the core of who we are comes from the divine image—or to apply it more personally, the divine *imprint*.

It is the divine imprint that allows all other matters pertaining to identity to fall into place. I discovered that "blackness," as a racial and cultural distinctive, was an expression of God's creation; however, it was not the core of my identity. God's imprint is the core of my identity. This reality freed me to appreciate the richness and beauty of my cultural heritage, and simultaneously to silence the self-loathing and conflicting messages that had tormented me from my adolescent years.

In our highly racialized world, at a time in life when the pressing issue is a quest for identity (answering the question "Who am I?"), youth desperately need to discover their divine imprint.

Leave Nothing Behind

Shortly after entering urban youth ministry, I was asked to participate in a workshop at a suburban church missions conference. My co-facilitator was one of the few black members of that church. As we talked prior to the workshop, it became clear that he was deeply conflicted. He talked about his childhood. "My father kept a shotgun by the front door. . . . It was a dangerous place. I could never go back to a neighborhood like that. Never!" He became so agitated that he left. I led the workshop on my own.

For many blacks, a return to the inner city would be something like a Jew returning to life in a concentration camp. A generation of blacks fled the city never to return, except possibly for a few nostalgic hours on Sunday morning for church. That could easily have been me. But once I accepted that the inner city might be God's calling upon my life, I knew I had to deal with some unresolved issues—the scars born out of growing up urban.

James is one of the most direct and blunt of all the apostles. The opening line of his letter can feel at once like a joyful command and a jarring slap across the face:

> Consider it pure joy, my brothers and sisters, whenever you face trials of many kinds, because you know that the testing of your faith produces perseverance. Let perseverance finish its work so that you may be mature and complete, not lacking anything (James 1:2-4).

Most Christians spend so much time reflecting (or agonizing) over the first part of this passage that they fail to consider the last part. The phrase "not lacking anything" literally means: "leaving nothing behind." In order to grow to maturity in Christ, nothing—no unresolved issue, lingering anger, or confusion regarding one's identity—can be left behind.

God has an ingenious method for addressing unresolved issues: trials. There is something about trials that bring to light the things we have tried to leave behind. It is a sobering truth: We take our problems with us.

Whatever personal issues you brought to bear on your last job, if they remain unresolved, will show up and contribute to disruption at your next job. James says that's a good thing: God's goal for us is maturity and completeness, and He will use trials to give us as many opportunities as it takes to straighten us out.

Now, I'm not saying that we should try to create trials for one another so that we all have more opportunities to deal with our issues. But I do believe that youth ministry can and should create an environment in which adolescents can begin to address those areas that might hold them back in life. Most urban youth I meet have already spent significant time surviving the harshness of the city. They carry with them the baggage of street ideas, survival tactics, suspicions and fears regarding life. A youth ministry should be a place where Jesus can heal those deep, life-shaping wounds.

Discerning Truth

Jesus put a high premium on truth when He said, "If you hold to my teaching, you are really my disciples. Then you will know the truth, and the truth will set you free" (John 8:31-32). Perhaps you recall my fellow seminarian John Peyton. John's gift to me was that of honest, truthful confrontation. Here were two people, coming from different perspectives, each possessing a deep love for Jesus. That bond of love allowed us to enter into rich debate: He challenged the socks off of me, and I did the same for him. The experience was life giving and life changing.

Pastor and theologian Haddon Robinson has said, "If you're going to compete for the minds of men and women"—and adolescents, I would add—"you must do so in the realm of ideas." Our society has become increasingly partisan. People now entrench themselves on differing sides of issues. Assertion has become the dominant posture; winning arguments has become more important than discerning truth. Now more than ever, young people need places where honest questions can dare to be spoken and honest answers can be pursued with loving integrity. Because knowing Jesus leads to truth, the pursuit of truth can also lead back to Jesus. This should characterize youth ministry: a safe environment where, as Francis Schaeffer put it, honest answers can be given to honest questions.

A Purposeful Journey

I sometimes challenge youth workers with the question, "When you look at young people, what do you see?" Their responses often highlight the hardening of urban youths' lives and the seemingly insurmountable task of breaking through that hardness with the gospel. I listen to their impressions, and then I share with them this story.

One day a construction foreman decided to take a walk through the building site. He would stop periodically and ask his men what they were doing.

One replied, "I'm breaking rocks."

Another said, "I'm earning a living to take care of my family."

Then he posed the question to a third worker. With a glint in his eyes, this man responded, "I'm building a cathedral."

At this point, I repeat the question, "When you look at youth, what do you see? Rocks? Employment? *Or do you see cathedrals in the making?*" Then I add, "Which one do you suppose God wants you to see?"

My three-plus decades of ministry among urban youth were not entered into by happenstance. They were the outflow of an ongoing story. The events of my life seemed ordinary and disconnected until I saw them from God's perspective. Once I began to do that, they formed a bigger picture—a more purposeful tapestry.

From other vantage points, an operatically trained kid who fled the city and was later converted to Christianity in a European cultural center would be a poor choice for an urban youth leader. But then again, perhaps a person like that might see things others would tend to miss, bringing to the table a new perspective on the urban youth challenge and the role the church can play in meeting it.

I certainly hope so.

Notes

1. *New Oxford American Dictionary*, Third Edition (New York: Oxford University Press, 2010).

2. John Baillie, *A Diary of Private Prayer* (New York: Touchstone, 2010), Kindle edition.

Questions for Thought

1. How has the hand of God worked in your life? How would you describe the pattern your life has been weaving?

2. Are you prepared to enter into the life experience of the urban young person?

3. Are there unresolved issues in your life related to identity? (Young people can spot phoniness almost immediately. They will know if you are asking Jesus to do something in their lives you have not allowed Him to do in yours.)

4. When you look at young people, what do you see? Rocks? Employment? Cathedrals? How do you think God wants you to view the youth in your community?

Chapter 5

TRANSFORMATION

*Your great glory is not to be inferior
to what God has made you.*

PERICLES

❝Ted, I hear you've left Youth for Christ to start a new ministry. Let's get together for coffee.❞

I counted it a privilege to have Rick as a friend. A former NFL player, he was big and gregarious, with a heart of gold.

"Well, buddy, you've done it! You have pulled the trigger and now you are committed to building this new ministry. So here are some things I think you need to do . . ."

Rick's advice was strong and sincere: "Here are some 'deep pocket' potential donors you should approach." "You should consider partnering with [this other ministry]." "You should talk to [this person] about serving on your board." I appreciated his advice but was unsettled as to how some of his directives fit with the ministry I was envisioning.

Perhaps it was my youthful idealism and my eagerness to go where others feared to tread. More likely, observers saw a crazed person engaged in a noble yet impossible task and desperately in need of all the help he could get. I had moved into Five Points intent on creating a community-based youth ministry. That action prompted not only Rick but also many other friends who were leaders in their own right to weigh in.

Throughout my life, I have been blessed with great friends and wise leaders. I appreciate their concern for me and their desire to help me along the way. But you have to be careful with free advice. A wise man once said, "Listen to others, but hold your own counsel." It is important to listen to advice, to glean from the wisdom and experiences of those who care about you. But when all is said and done, you alone must decide and define.

I knew my friends who gave advice early on genuinely wanted me to succeed. But I had to reject some of their counsel because my friends' perceptions of the ministerial task did not align with my own. I discovered early in the journey the importance of *definition*: If you do not clearly define who you are, what you are doing and why, others—without even realizing it—will impose their agendas on you. Businessman and leadership author Max De Pree was profoundly on target when he declared: "The first task of leadership is to define reality."

Definition does not come easy. One of the most difficult sentences to write is a purpose statement. During the first two decades of Neighborhood Ministries' existence, our statement was revised numerous times. Why? It took time to find the right combination of words to capture what we believed God wanted us to do. A mission statement should reflect a singular purpose and clarify your organization's unique reason for being. Honing that statement takes time.

Over time, our work evolved into a clear philosophy of ministry and process of urban youth development. Until recently I had no name for it.

Now I call it transformational discipleship. When I first settled on this terminology, I thought I had discovered something original. But self-congratulations ended the moment I Googled the phrase. Books had been written a decade ago titled *Transformational Discipleship* and *Transforming Discipleship*. I even found an online assessment tool by that name! As with many words wrung through the Christian cultural mill, I discovered that the words "transformation" and "discipleship" had been frequently used, both separately and together, for some time.

Have they outlived their usefulness? I wondered. *Perhaps I should find a different name.* But I could not let the phrase "transformational discipleship" go. It captured perfectly the essence of the concept I was attempting to convey. Separately, each term highlighted a significant dimension of the ministry process. Together, they introduced a dynamic and unique approach to urban youth development.

About Transformation

> I will give you a new heart and put a new spirit in you; I will remove from you your heart of stone and give you a heart of flesh (Ezekiel 36:26).

The word "transform" holds special significance within Christian thought and practice. The dictionary defines the verb this way: "To make a thorough or dramatic change in the form, appearance, or character of."[1] A transliteration from the Greek gives us the word *metamorphosis*.

There are three places in the Scriptures where this word is used. The first is in Matthew's description of Jesus' Transfiguration.

> After six days Jesus took with him Peter, James and John the brother of James, and led them up a high mountain by themselves. There he was transfigured before them. His face shone like the sun, and his clothes became as white as the light (Matthew 17:1-2).

The Wuest translation reads: "the manner of his outward expression was changed before them, and his face shone as the sun."

Jesus was God *incarnate*—that is, embodied in flesh, in human form. Of Him the Scriptures say, "The Word became flesh and made his dwelling among us" (John 1:14) and "He made himself nothing by taking the very nature of a servant, being made in human likeness" (Phil. 2:7). Jesus publicly appeared as a man—the Son of Man. But that day on the mountain, in the presence of His closest disciples, Jesus allowed His true essence—the Son of God—to show.

Paul later used the same term (on two separate occasions) to describe the dynamic and ongoing experience of the believer:

> Do not conform to the pattern of this world, but be transformed by the renewing of your mind. Then you will be able to test and approve what God's will is—his good, pleasing and perfect will (Romans 12:2).

> And we all, who with unveiled faces contemplate the Lord's glory, are being transformed into his image with ever-increasing glory, which comes from the Lord, who is the Spirit (2 Corinthians 3:18).

What do these two passages tell us about transformation?

- To be transformed is to experience a dramatic change in behavior.
- Transformative change begins with the renewal (renovation, complete change for the better) of the mind (one's thinking processes). Tom Skinner would say, "It's not 'since Jesus entered my heart,' but 'since Jesus entered my *mind.*'"
- For the believer, transformation is both commanded and expected. The emphasis in Paul's exhortation to the Romans is: *allow yourself* to be changed by the renewing of your mind.

Preaching Is Not Enough

If you were to break down the average youth ministry into its component parts, you would find—in addition to copious amounts of pizza, games and music—a significant dose of preaching. By "preaching" I mean one-way communication (whether it comes from a pulpit or from one of a dozen folding chairs arranged in a circle in a fellowship hall). Now exhortation is a powerful mode of persuasion that has resulted in changed lives. Preaching can indeed trigger transformation, but only when two other factors are present: the engaged mind of the listener, and a heart that is open to change.

One Sunday I attended a church service where the guest preacher was the congregation's former pastor. He spoke with great passion and animation. He shared colorful illustrations and funny stories. People seemed delighted to hear him again.

During the fellowship hour, I remarked how impressed I was. A longtime member of the church overheard me. She said dryly: "You wouldn't feel that way if you had to sit through that same message and those same stories Sunday after Sunday. That's what we got for years!"

I'm sure that preacher loved his former flock. He wanted to "bless" them through his ministry. But something was missing. Few of his statements were designed to induce change from within. His message was laced with anecdotes and clichés that he had used repeatedly during his tenure as pastor. The congregation, as if on cue, shouted: "Amen!" They were entertained—but they were not transformed.

The great Danish philosopher Søren Kierkegaard humorously illustrates this principle in his well-known Parable of the Ducks:

A story is told of a town where all the residents are ducks. Every Sunday the ducks waddle out of their houses and waddle down Main Street to their church. They waddle into the sanctuary and squat in their proper pews.

The duck choir waddles in and takes its place, and then the duck minister comes forward and opens the duck Bible. He reads to them: "Ducks! God has given you wings! With wings you can fly! With wings you can mount up and soar like eagles. No walls can confine you! No fences can hold you! You have wings. God has given you wings, and you can fly like birds!"

All the ducks shout, "Amen!" *And then they all waddle home.*

Variations on this theme often show up in youth meetings. The strategy employed is persuasion through assertion. Those in the audience who are already convinced (pastors, adult youth staff, other Christian onlookers) heartily affirm the message. But post-Christian youth feel they have heard these clichés *ad infinitum*. Hearing them again—with no relevant contextualization or practical application—amounts to a brazen attempt at coercion.

The gospel is good news—the greatest anyone this side of heaven will ever hear! We feel Paul's urgency: "Woe to me if I do not preach the gospel!" (1 Corinthians 9:16). Yet Paul did not sacrifice reason on the altar of fervency. He knew that if transformation was going to take place, the mind first had to be renewed. His exhortation to the Roman church on this topic stemmed from his firsthand experience and observation of the transforming power of God's Word:

- After his conversion, Paul spent 15 years in Tarsus preparing for future ministry. He reprocessed everything he knew about God through the new grid of knowing Christ. He let the gospel transform his life and his message.
- Paul did not treat the gospel message as an incantation possessing magical powers. When Isaiah declared: "It [God's word] will not return to me empty, but will accomplish what I desire and achieve the purpose for which I sent it" (Isaiah 55:11), he was not saying that his words were magical, but rather that they were effective and filled

with grace. The gospel is "the power of God that brings salvation" (Romans 1:16), but words themselves are not magical. Words are as powerful as the *ideas* they convey. Paul mastered the Kingdom ideas (truths) that undergirded his message.

- Paul engaged people with those ideas. "We demolish arguments and every pretension that sets itself up against the knowledge of God, and we take captive every thought to make it obedient to Christ" (2 Corinthians 10:5). He fought to win the battle for people's minds.

- He was adept at reasoning, appealing to people's understanding. King Agrippa found Paul's arguments to be so compelling that he cried out: "Do you think that in such a short time you can persuade me to be a Christian?" (Acts 26:28). To which Paul replied, "Short time or long—I pray to God that not only you but all who are listening to me today may become what I am, except for these chains" (v. 29).

So Christian transformation begins when gospel ideas, empowered by God's grace, take root in people's minds. Such ideas then lead to behaviors consistent with those ideas. When Paul exhorted the Corinthian believers to "imitate me, just as I also imitate Christ" (1 Corinthians 11:1, *NKJV*), he was highlighting both his belief system and the behaviors those beliefs produced.

The Medium Is the Message

The pursuit of transformation involves not only the engaging of ideas but also the use of appropriate methods.

Careful study of Paul's movements reveals that he employed strategies consistent with his mission. He targeted cities, knowing the gospel would spread outward to the rural areas. His methods mirrored the incarnation (i.e., Jesus' choice to become human and dwell among those He had come to love and serve): Paul stayed in people's homes, interacted with local residents in synagogues and public squares, gathered converts around him, and demonstrated by his own behavior the things he taught.

This incorporating of beliefs into organizational behavior, ensuring that operations clearly reflect core values, is where many ministries fall short. Here are some of the missteps:

- Some "helping ministries" do more harm than good. In the short run, ministries like youth mentoring programs, food basket giveaways, and short-term mission projects provide welcome relief. But the damage to people's dignity can be devastating. If these types of programs are not approached carefully, black youth will catch the subtle message that only white people can solve their problems. A father's shame goes unnoticed as he watches his children open Christmas gifts provided by wealthy strangers. Poor churches become dependent on the resources of foreigners, snuffing out any personal motivation to solve their own problems.

- Jesus never issued "blind" orders to His disciples. His demeanor was not: "Do this, and don't ask why; just do it!" He valued transparency and informed participation. "I have called you friends, for everything that I learned from my Father I have made known to you" (John 15:15). As Merrill C. Tenney writes in his commentary: "Jesus elevated the disciples above mere tools and made them partners in his work. A slave is never given a reason for the work assigned to him; he must perform it because he has no other choice. The friend is a confidant who shares the knowledge of his superior's purpose and voluntarily adopts it as his own."[2] This is servant leadership, a quality sorely missing in many Christian organizations today.

Behaviors send a powerful message, for they convey our true beliefs. Hence the saying: "What you are doing speaks so loudly I cannot hear what you are saying." When methods sync with ideas, the message is credible. When they do not, the message is suspect, and transformation is stifled.

Transformation and Leadership

In their groundbreaking book *Transformational Leadership*, Bernard Bass and Ronald Riggio examine the differences between transactional and transformational leadership. Let me explain.

Transactional leaders focus on managing exchanges. Politicians exchange jobs for votes. Bosses offer financial incentives for productivity. The leader defines what is required and then specifies conditions and rewards related to the transaction. Motivation for productivity is *external*: the jobs, the paycheck, the perks.

All leadership engages in transactions. But transformational leadership operates at a much higher level. Transformational leaders are characterized by:

- *Charisma*: They behave in ways that allow them to serve as role models.
- *Inspiration*: They behave in ways that motivate and inspire others by pressing meaning and challenge into their work.
- *Intellectual stimulation*: They stimulate followers to be innovative and creative; they encourage the questioning of assumptions, the reframing of problems, and approaching old situations in new ways.
- *Individual consideration*: They pay special attention to the individual follower's need for achievement and growth. They serve by acting as a coach or mentor.[3]

Transformational leaders focus on tapping *internal* motivations; they *induce* (engender, encourage, trigger) change in others.

In the workplace, such leadership manifests itself through: (1) commitment to a vision that is shared by the team, (2) innovative problem solving, and (3) maximizing the individual's leadership potential.

The Power of Aptness

Among their other characteristics, transformational leaders are keenly aware of the power that can be wielded through words. The right words spoken at the right time can produce life-changing results. The Bible has a name for this: aptness.

> A person finds joy in giving an apt reply—and how good is a timely word! (Proverbs 15:23).

Aptness is the quality of being appropriate or suitable.[4] Jesus was a master at cutting through fuzzy thinking with clear teaching that spoke directly to people's deepest needs and most pressing questions. We see this in His encounters with Nicodemus and the Samaritan woman (see John 3, 4). He not only spoke truth; He also spoke it aptly. He was adept at expressing the right idea at the right time.

Commenting on Proverbs, Bible scholar Derek Kidner explains: "A truth that in general makes no impression may be indelibly fixed in the mind when it is matched to its occasion and shaped to its task."[5]

Aptness is a tool of transformation. It touches the mind.

Recently I was in court with a friend who was fighting for custody of his children. Another minister and I were sitting outside the courtroom, talking with this friend's 12-year-old daughter. Cute and spunky, she went on and on about how she could never forgive this other person who had done her wrong.

After listening awhile to her stubborn insistence that she was right, despite the reasoning of the other pastor, I commented: "Only forgiven people forgive." My friend's daughter was taken aback (to my surprise, so was the pastor!).

"What do you mean?" she asked.

I explained: "If you've never tasted God's forgiveness, you won't be able to forgive. If you have tasted God's forgiveness for the bad things you've done, you'll be able to forgive the bad things others have done to you. Only forgiven people forgive."

That simple comment jarred her thinking and prompted her to ponder what her refusal to forgive said about her own experience of God's grace.

I have also found myself on the receiving end of apt words. When I began my seminary education, I had little interest in urban ministry. I was convinced God was fine with me not serving in the inner city. I was making this point rather fervently to some students in the hallway one day, not realizing that Dr. Vernon Grounds, the seminary president, was standing (lurking!) nearby.

I must have said something like "I'm not responsible . . ." when a voice rang out: "Are you *sure*? Are you *sure* you're not responsible?" as Dr. Grounds passed by and disappeared up the stairway.

That simple, passing question stopped me in my tracks. It hounded me! A few months later, I found myself volunteering at a storefront mission in Five Points. My journey into the city had begun, thanks to an apt word that challenged my thinking on an important topic.

Inducing change requires more than pronouncements. It requires aptness: ideas that compel the listener to change because they speak directly to a felt need.

So the "transformational" side of transformational discipleship has to do with change—change that results not by coercion or force, but through the influence of Kingdom ideas upon thought patterns, perspectives and beliefs. Changes in thought lead to changes in behavior—and that is transformation. A transformational ministry is not careless about its methods, as if the end justified the means. Its methods—addressing felt needs, maximizing potential, pressing core values into organizational policy and practice, the apt response—are intentionally transformational as well.

Whereas the term "transformational" addresses the dynamics of *change*, "discipleship" speaks to the *environment* needed for change to take place.

About Discipleship

My years in Vienna, under the tutelage of my pastor, missionaries and newfound Christian friends, were formative ones. They were discipleship intensive. Everything—friendships, the counsel and instruction I received, my meager leadership exerted toward youth in the International School, the many struggles and failures—played a foundational role in my early spiritual growth and formation.

Yet until recently, if you asked me how I had been discipled, I would point to a 10-week Wednesday evening class taught by a missionary from the Navigators, an international discipleship ministry. The instructor of this class employed what is known today as *Design for Discipleship*, an excellent curriculum I've used many times over the years.

Why did I single out that class as "discipleship," to the exclusion of the other events that had shaped my life? Like many others, I had adopted a fairly academic definition of discipleship, in which the central activity was the acquisition of knowledge about God and His Word. To be sure, learning Christian content is a significant part of being discipled. But being trained and nurtured as a follower of Jesus extends far beyond any formal classroom.

I cannot imagine categorizing Jesus' sermons as "discipleship" while viewing His responses to individuals and situations merely as "teachable moments." Discipleship is not the same as a catechism class. Discipleship is learning and applying Christian content in the context of life.

Consider what Eugene Peterson, translator of *THE MESSAGE* and author of *A Long Obedience in the Same Direction*, writes on the subject:

Disciple . . . says we are people who spend our lives apprenticed to our master, Jesus Christ. We are in a growing-learning relationship, always. A disciple is a learner, but not in the academic setting of a schoolroom, rather at the work site of a craftsman. We do not acquire information about God but skills in faith.[6]

Discipleship is "a growing-learning relationship, always." This has sweeping implications for youth ministry. Many treat this ministry as a vehicle for evangelism. Conversion is viewed as the main goal to be reached, with discipleship as "icing on the cake." But even salvation is expressed in the Scriptures as having three dimensions: I *have been* saved, I *am being* saved, I *shall be* saved. Salvation is more than a point of entry; it is a process and also the final destination of the believer.

What if we dared to apply the command "Go and make disciples of all nations" (Matthew 28:19) to youth ministry? Might we be compelled to approach youth gatherings not as evangelistic military strikes but as part of a larger, sustained discipleship culture?

You see, these urban youth—those touched by brokenness yet bearing God's image—need a culture of discipleship. They need to be challenged to think—to ponder ideas bigger than those of the street. And they need a safe space where they can do so freely, openly and regularly.

As I considered discipleship, a paradigm shift took place within me. My assessments of young people had moved from "saved" versus "not saved" to "disciple", "not yet a disciple," and "open to becoming a disciple." My longing became to influence world views—to listen carefully and then challenge how youth interpreted life. With eyes open to who they were, I became focused on who, in Christ, they could become.

What are some key elements of this discipleship culture we need to create for our young people?

- Providing a steady witness as Christian leaders whose lives are transparent, accessible, and worthy of imitation ("Imitate me, just as I also imitate Christ" [1 Corinthians 11:1, *NKJV*]).
- Matching youths' natural search for meaning with the discovery of God's purpose for their lives.
- Ensuring that the Bible—the written Word that reveals God, the Living Word—is central to our process of discerning and understanding life. (Always exploring the question, Where is God in all this?)
- Learning by doing, where serving others becomes the classroom in which youth discover God and themselves, and in doing so are transformed.

The Wineskin Challenge

Jesus' parable regarding wineskins introduces the modern-day reader to a slice of life from the ancient world, where flasks were made out of goatskins. New skins, still soft and pliable, could hold fermenting wine. Pouring new wine into an old wineskin placed fermenting gases in a container that had become hard and brittle, causing that container to break. New wine, needing room to expand, required new wineskins.

As Jesus said "No one pours new wine into old wineskins. Otherwise, the new wine will burst the skins; the wine will run out and the wineskins will be ruined. No, new wine must be poured into new wineskins" (Luke 5:37-38).

The same is true for new ideas. Just as the gospel requires "new skin"—that is, new patterns of conduct consistent with Jesus' teachings on Kingdom life—so too must other new ideas be implemented within frameworks that are fresh and flexible enough to hold them. Transformational discipleship establishes a context for youth development in which certain skills and values glossed over in traditional approaches become paramount for effectiveness and success.

Such change does not come easily. Jesus warned: "And no one after drinking old wine wants the new, for they say, 'The old is better'" (Luke 5:39).

Like fermenting wine exerting pressure on an old wineskin, Jesus' teaching cannot be contained within an old religious system. It requires a new system—a new context. Yet Jesus acknowledges a sobering truth: People tend to resist the new—no matter how good it may be—in favor of the old.

Despite the skepticism and resistance we have sometimes encountered along the way, at Neighborhood Ministries we have embraced transformational discipleship as a new ministry context—new wineskins—to hold these key principles:

- As already described, the shift from an evangelistic focus to creating an environment conducive to knowing Christ and growing in Him.
- The shift from exerting authority on the basis of age, rank or title to yielding the kind of authority that emanates from one's character (see 1 Timothy 4:12) and commitment to the ongoing growth in Christ of the youth being served (see James 1:2-4).
- Visionary leadership that says to youth: "There's nothing you see in me that you cannot become" (transparency; credible role modeling; vision casting).
- Enacting organizational policies and practices that are congruent with the transformational discipleship philosophy and mission.

Embracing TransformationalDiscipleship

Transformational discipleship is an approach to youth ministry centered on maximizing the adolescent leadership experience in ways that mold youth for future service and motivate the future leaders (children) they influence.

1. An Approach

Transformational discipleship is first of all *an approach to youth ministry.*

Youth programs come in all shapes and sizes. But generally speaking, they encompass three age groups: children, early adolescents and adolescents. Youth ministries tend to mirror the organizational structure found in secular educational institutions. Each "grade" receives a focus all its own, separate from the other age groups, resulting in distinct, age-related curricula.

Children ▶ **Early Adolescents** ▶ **Adolescents** ▶

This model is characterized by a lack of interrelating between age groups. Because the context is the classroom, and each class is age-specific, there is little influence of older children on younger ones.

Transformational discipleship builds on the oft-quoted African proverb: "It takes a village to raise a child." In villages, children influence one another: Older children have responsibility for the younger, and the younger can envision their future by observing the older.

Transformational discipleship capitalizes on the natural desire of youth to influence children by involving adolescents in the development process of younger children. In a carefully designed leadership environment, adolescents engage in teaching and leading children, and while doing so learn about God and themselves.

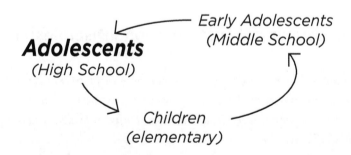

2. Leadership

Transformational discipleship *maximizes the adolescent leadership experience*. It invites youth to join a leadership team that takes responsibility for ministry to younger children.

On a transactional level, these youth are accomplishing a task: teach children and lead the children's program. But from a transformational perspective, the "job" becomes an opportunity to discover, develop and exercise their unique talents. The problems, challenges and roadblocks inherent in any meaningful endeavor become teachable moments—opportunities for supportive adults to explain and help process youth leaders' experiences in order to arrive at best solutions. Through these experiences, the youth learn about God and themselves, in the real-life context of meaningful service.

Within this discipleship-rich environment, adult leaders serve as coaches and mentors (not preachers or drill sergeants).

3. Direction

Transformational discipleship *molds adolescents (emerging leaders) for future service*. It addresses the question: What is the church's responsibility to young people during the formative years of their lives?

At a time when their greatest quest is for identity (answering the question, "Who am I?"), leadership helps adolescents discover the divine imprint—the uniqueness of their creation. Over time, they gain appreciation for their strengths, as they gravitate toward helping to meet those needs for which they sense they are particularly qualified. Awareness of personal strengths, reinforced through meaningful service, helps direct adolescents toward fulfilling tasks, jobs and vocations that maximize their gifts and abilities.

4. Legacy

Transformational discipleship *motivates the future leaders (children) the emerging leaders influence*. Something very powerful happens when credible role models only a few years older in age lead children. Often, during our summer day camp, a child would approach me and ask, "Can I do what they [the emerging leaders] are doing someday?" One of many positive outcomes of transformational discipleship is children aspiring to lead.

In a social context saturated with violence and brokenness, adolescent disciples of Jesus bring real hope to children. In these young leaders, children can recognize positive possibilities for their lives. As for the leaders, they experience what Jesus promised: "It is more blessed to give than to receive" (Acts 20:35). Through their acts of service, they simultaneously influence the next generation of emerging leaders, position themselves for a variety of educational and vocational opportunities, and leave a precious legacy in their communities.

Something Special Is Happening Here

The emerging leaders had completed their four months of preparation. Now they were well into the second week of the Summer Enrichment Program (our five-week summer day camp for third-through fifth-grade neighborhood kids). A seminary student was interested in doing an internship with Neighborhood Ministries, and he had asked to meet with me. I invited him to have lunch with me at the camp.

I had caught glimpses of the fruit of our approach to youth development prior to that lunch. I saw it during the training as the emerging leaders infused their unique ideas into the camp program. I witnessed it in their excitement at preparing Bible studies and decorating their learning center classrooms. They did more than work at the camp: They seemed to own it.

But it was while observing the lunchroom that I began to fathom the significance of this transformational discipleship approach. My guest and I had arrived early, so we had already grabbed plates of food that had been prepared by a team of volunteers and had sat down at a table along the wall when the campers began to file in.

What happened next seemed at first rather ordinary. Kids and teenage staff picked up their plates and sat down at the tables. There was talking and laughter. The campers seemed relaxed as they enjoyed their food and one another's company. After a while, I noticed the staff rise and go to the serving table, where the volunteers had prepared dessert. The staff took the dessert to the campers! After serving them, the staff quietly rejoined the campers. The only sound that remained constant was mild chatter and laughter, which was finally interrupted by Raquel's announcement that lunchtime was over.

It seemed an ordinary event until we—the seminary student and I—began to explore the question, Why? Why were the kids so relaxed? Why was there such rapport between children and teenagers? We had both experienced meals with large groups of children before. One expects a few chaotic bursts to occur. Why did this meal go so smoothly?

That is when I recognized the extent to which we had successfully taken the lessons learned over the past 20 years and pressed them into an approach to youth development that actually transformed lives. The fruit of that approach was on display at lunch, in the attitudes and behaviors of the kids and staff.

I overheard a parent remark after observing the camp: "There's something special going on here."

It *was* special. Transformational discipleship was happening in our midst.

Notes

1. *New Oxford American Dictionary*, Third Edition (New York: Oxford University Press, 2010).
2. Frank E. Gaebelein, ed., *Expositor's Bible Commentary*, Vol. 9: John and Acts (Grand Rapids, MI: Zondervan, 1984), p. 151.
3. Bernard M. Bass and Ronald E. Riggio, *Transformational Leadership* (Mahwah, NJ: Lawrence Erlbaum Associates, 2006), Kindle edition.
4. *New Oxford American Dictionary*.
5. Derek Kidner, *Tyndale Old Testament Commentaries*, Vol. 17 (Carol Stream, IL: Tyndale Press, 1964), "Proverbs 15:13."
6. Eugene Peterson, *A Long Obedience in the Same Direction* (Downers Grove, IL: IVP Books, 2012), Kindle edition.

Questions for Thought

1. What is transactional and what is transformational about your current leadership style and practices? To strengthen the transformational dimension of your leadership, what needs to change?

2. How would you describe the culture of your youth ministry? What steps can be taken to create more of a discipleship environment?

3. What "wineskin" challenges are you facing? How can you work to create a fresh ministry context in which new ideas can flourish?

Foundations

Why Transformational Discipleship?

It took me years of ministry among youth to discover (or stumble into) this philosophy of ministry, which has since developed into what I call a strategic construct.

A construct is an idea or theory formed by multiple elements. I did not realize the need for such a construct until, as a doctoral student at the Bakke Graduate School of Ministry, I explored the research question, How can the church animate (bring to life) leadership capacity among youth native to higher-risk communities?

Few scholars or ministry leaders had addressed the subject. Those who did were highly theoretical, offering little practical insight.

Yet I needed to answer the question, Why transformational discipleship? So I framed the answer as a construct—the coming together of four separate yet related concepts:

1. *Mission* as the identity and purpose of the church;
2. *Urban youth* as a focus of neighbor love and discipleship;
3. *The image of God* as key to personal motivation and life contribution; and
4. *Leadership* as the activity in which discipleship, image discovery and life purpose come alive during the adolescent years.

The following section examines these foundational concepts. I realize that theological concepts can come across as a bit heady. My desire is the same as that implied in the title of Dr. Bruce Shelley's masterful work: *Church History in Plain Language*. Hopefully I have achieved that goal in answering the why of transformational discipleship.

I am also aware that reading these chapters might require a measure of courage. If my theology and reasoning are sound, the material presented here may prompt a dramatic change in thinking and behavior. It could cause you—as it has done me—never to see work among urban youth the same way again.

So my prayer for you is courage—courage to discern and act upon the implications of God's Word to your life and ministry.

> Have I not commanded you? Be strong and courageous.
> Do not be afraid; do not be discouraged, for the LORD your
> God will be with you wherever you go (Joshua 1:9).

Chapter 6

MISSION

TIME TO BRING MISSION HOME

I should have been excited. I was studying mission in China as a doctoral student. But I was consumed by problems at home.

The forces of gentrification and migration had altered the landscape of my community. Yuppies and new immigrants were displacing families our ministry had served for years. It was as if the foundation had been ripped out from under us. How were we as a ministry to respond? Should the ministry move with the people being displaced? What were we going to do?

Far from being exciting, China felt like a distraction. "What am I doing here?" I agonized. "How can being in Hong Kong help address my problems back in teeny-tiny Denver?" (China makes most American cities look teeny-tiny.)

Toward the end of my time in China, the answer came: perspective.

From within my community, I could see and feel changes coming at me, but I could not understand the what or the why. I could not see the forest for the trees. But from 7,000 miles away, I gained perspective.

From the vantage point of China (and with the help of professors such as Ray Bakke), I realized that I was experiencing what everyone on the planet was experiencing: the greatest global migration in the history of the world. People in the southern hemisphere were heading northward, the "have-nots" were moving toward the "haves," and the phenomenon of gentrification had uprooted the poor in cities throughout the United States and the Western world.

This great global shift was behind the tsunami engulfing my neighborhood. It had taken me and other urban leaders by surprise. But it had not surprised or stymied God. God knew exactly what was going on, because He has been behind all the great migrations of the world. Something big was happening. The global playing field was changing. And God was in it.

As I considered these things, I deeply appreciated the insights Ray Bakke shared about mission and what it is today. There was a time when mission was about the missionary—those brave souls who would leave the comforts of America to serve in foreign lands. Mission was something embarked on by the chosen few, and it happened "over there"—not locally, but somewhere far away.

But now the mission paradigm has shifted; God has brought the world to our cities. Now the foreigner is our neighbor; mission has come to us. "We have left the world of the missionary," Bakke declared, "and entered the world of mission."

This world of mission is one we should never have left.

We Are Witnesses

He [Jesus] said to them, "This is what I told you while I was still with you: Everything must be fulfilled that is written about me in the Law of Moses, the Prophets and the Psalms."

Then he opened their minds so they could understand the Scriptures. He told them, "This is what is written: The Messiah will suffer and rise from the dead on the third day, and repentance for the forgiveness of sins will be preached in his name to all nations, beginning at Jerusalem. You are witnesses of these things. I am going to send you what my

Father has promised; but stay in the city until you have been clothed with power from on high" (Luke 24:44-49).

Luke 24 is the final chapter of Luke's "carefully investigated. . . orderly account" of the life of Jesus (Luke 1:3). Here he describes the post-resurrection encounter that led the disciples to full recognition that Jesus is the Christ. Luke also leads us, his readers, to a dramatic conclusion regarding Christian identity and purpose. That purpose is captured in the word "witness" (Luke 24:48). Jesus' followers (then and now) are to be witnesses—missionaries— and will be empowered to do so after receiving "what the Father has promised" (i.e., the Spirit; see Luke 12:12 and Acts 1:8).

This "witness" is to the love of a God who is *concerned for the whole person*. Ray Bakke, reflecting on the early chapters of Genesis, notes that "God's hands are in the mud." Not only did He create mankind out of dirt, but He also chose to occupy human flesh Himself, both as the Messiah and through the Holy Spirit who indwells believers. "Christianity is the most materialistic religion on the entire earth," Bakke writes. "It's the only religion that successfully integrates matter and spirit with integrity."[1]

This "witness" is to the love of a God who is *urban*. That's right, Jesus was urban! The historian Josephus describes the Galilee of Jesus' day as a heavily populated area, known for exporting wheat, olives and wine. It was 30 to 40 kilometers in diameter, with a population numbering between 200,000 and 300,000.[2] The Bible tells us that Jesus went into the towns and villages throughout Galilee— an area encompassing 200 cities.

Why the disciples as apostles could transition so easily from Palestine to the cities of Rome's empire can now be understood. The disciples were not so parochial or so "pale" as we might have supposed. They were prepared to follow Jesus in an urbanized world, because that is where and how they were discipled. They were multi-environmental people. . . .

Even Judaism in the Palestinian or Diaspora variety was far more pluralistic than we can possibly imagine today.[3]

Finally, this "witness" is to a loving God who is *missional*. In his book *Transforming Mission: Paradigm Shifts in Theology of Mission*, David Bosch defines mission as the participation of the Christian community in the ongoing work of the living Christ, as witnesses and pointers to the love of God for the sake of the world.[4] This understanding of mission has profound implications for the church:

- The reign (Kingdom) of God is to be a central passion of the entire Christian community. Christ's work is ongoing, and it is accomplished through the church—God's people. When we pray, "Your kingdom come, your will be done, on earth as it is in heaven" (Matthew 6:10), we are not just asking God to make that which is up there (His reign, control, dominion) come down here. We are committing ourselves to active participation and effort toward that end.

- Jesus' ministry—and therefore the church's ministry—has as its focus the bringing of God's reign to those on the margins of society: the poor, the suffering, widows, children, "tax collectors" and "sinners." It is a defining characteristic of the believer to have the marginalized on our radar. "Did not he who made me in the womb make them [the poor]? Did not the same one form us both within our mothers?" (Job 31:15). Participating in Jesus' ongoing ministry means that we too are to "bring good news to the poor" (Luke 4:18).

- To follow Jesus is to embrace a missionary discipleship. We are commissioned to "go and make disciples of all nations" (Matthew 28:19). Luke offers some additional specifics: "You will receive power when the Holy Spirit comes on you; and you will be my witnesses in Jerusalem, and in all Judea and Samaria, and to the ends of the earth" (Acts 1:8). Our identity as Christians is to be characterized by our commitment to bringing the good news of God's transforming love to whatever part of the world we find ourselves in. When Jesus states: "You are the salt of the earth. . . . You are the light of the world" (Matthew 5:13-16), the "you" is emphatic (*"You and you alone are . . ."*). This, Jesus declares, is your purpose—your destiny.

A Post-Modern World

Bosch's book was, for me, a perspective changer. Heady yet engaging, the text first guides readers through Matthew, Luke and Paul's rich description of mission as the purpose of the church. Bosch then embarks on a careful critique of the succeeding ages (the Eastern Orthodox, Medieval, Protestant Reformation, Enlightenment and then-emerging post-Modern eras) and how the church's purpose has been challenged—and at times compromised—by the societal pressures it faced.

Bosch highlights a sobering reality: No one chooses the time in which he or she lives. No one chooses his or her parents, relatives, culture or generation. But if you are Christian, you are purposed to be God's witness within the community-culture-nation-world-generation-epoch in which God has placed you.

"Therefore, since we are surrounded by such a great cloud of witnesses [the faithful listed in Hebrews 11], let us throw off everything that hinders and the sin that so easily entangles. And let us run with perseverance the race marked out for us, fixing our eyes on Jesus, the pioneer and perfecter of faith" (Hebrews 12:1-2).

Just as this cloud of witnesses referred to people from past generations, the exhortation reaches forward to every generation, including ours today. No matter the generation or culture, the church is mandated to fulfill its role as participants in the ongoing work of its Lord.

We live in a post-modern world. It is fair to say our society has grown increasingly nihilistic (rejecting religious and moral principles, instead believing that life is meaningless). The lines dividing order from disorder and right from wrong have been blurred. The view of life as having order and connectedness has been replaced by a view that treats life as snapshots, or situational short-stories. The result is a disconnect from truth, reason and stability. In the post-modern era, a concept of life as stable or permanent has all but disappeared.[5]

This state of affairs can be discouraging. Yet with change comes opportunity. This was Bosch's hope as he envisioned the missionary paradigm advocated by Matthew, Luke and Paul reemerging in a post-modern world.

- In this paradigm, the church would see itself as essentially missionary—a pilgrim people bound together as witnesses and pointers to Jesus and to the kingdom of God.
- In this paradigm, mission would no longer be viewed as one of many activities in the church, but as an attribute of God characterizing the entire church.
- In this paradigm, mission would demand a more comprehensive understanding of salvation, which includes both spiritual and physical renewal.
- Inherent in this paradigm would be a quest for justice and social transformation. "There is no room. . . for a gospel that is indifferent to the needs of the total man nor of the global man," said Carl F. H. Henry. Mission would require an authentic evangelism that flowed from an authentic lifestyle and included the preaching and practice of justice.[6]

Church Out of Context

Understanding the church's purpose as essentially missional marks a dramatic shift in Western Christian thought. The New Testament is clear: No Christian is exempt from the task of obeying, in the here and now, the simple command to love your neighbor (see Luke 10:27). Yet as stated before, we in the West have tended to view mission as the calling of a few to foreign lands, not as applying to us within our communities.

Reasons for this are sad but simple. Creating theologies that accommodate self-interest and self-preservation has been a recurring theme throughout history. It wasn't long ago that our nation justified the institution of slavery by deriving from the Bible a theological framework for its practice. Everyone—all manner of individuals, groups and cultures—has this tendency to see in the Bible only what they wish to see.

We are in the grip of one such human-contrived framework today: a framework designed to justify physical, social and economic isolation from society's poor. This perspective effectively blinds us to our call to mission, and with it the Kingdom-advancing moment that stands before us. It is as subtle as it is devious: the simple subordination of the Great Command ("love God and love your neighbor") to the Great Commission ("go and preach the gospel").

This wrong thinking is deeply embedded among evangelicals. If you believe that people without Christ are going to spend eternity in hell, then sharing the gospel becomes the most important and urgent of Christian tasks. About this there is no dispute! Yet, as Robert Lupton, in his book *Compassion, Justice and the Christian Life*, rightly observes, to allow the Great Commission to override the Great Command dangerously reduces people to "souls" in need of saving and compassion to an evangelistic technique.[7] In effect, subordinating the Great Command to the Great Commission has a corrupting effect on both the command and the commission!

Ray Bakke writes:

Under the pressure of a billion "lost souls". . . many overly pragmatic Western Christians have adopted a hierarchy of values—redemption over creation—for the sake of the evangelistic mandate. This hierarchy has created the great divorce (evangelism from social action) and resulted in a canon within the canon of Scriptures—that is, while they believe the whole Bible is the word of God, they treat certain parts as more valuable or useful than others.[8]

Think about it: This simple priority flip (elevating commission over command) has justified and fueled a church out of context—out of step with mission. We are certainly compelled to preach the gospel (see 1 Corinthians 9:16). But to share the gospel with someone from whom we have isolated ourselves in every other way—culturally, economically, socially—casts a shadow on the truthfulness of our message! We have convinced ourselves that what we say excuses how we live—that God approves when we distance ourselves from a brother or sister in need with the words: "God loves you; now 'go in peace; keep warm and well fed'" (James 2:16), and that the gospel need not be incarnated.

(This does not dismiss the many evangelistic efforts that are not incarnational. God has and will continue to use people like Billy Graham and Greg Laurie to reach the masses through their evangelistic campaigns. God can work through the use of gospel tracts to reach a stranger. But we do not live in stadia, nor should our lives consist solely of chance encounters. If we live in a neighborhood, we are commanded to love our neighbor.)

Years ago, prior to the great migrational changes we're experiencing today, I would exhort my suburban friends to consider moving into the inner city. Most thought I was crazy; for many, their response was similar to that of the wealthy man when Jesus told him to sell his possessions and give to the poor: They went away sad. Moving into the city was just too much to ask.

More recently, suburban church communities have experienced a dramatic increase in immigrants from Latin America, Asia, Africa and other places around the world. So today my message is different: Don't move! God has brought the poor of the world to you. Stay. Love your neighbors!

Many sincere believers fail to weigh the hundreds of references to the poor and cities in their daily reading of Scripture. Most Western Christians accept a commuter church lifestyle that allows them to drive by poor communities on their way to Sunday services and have minimal awareness or concern for the residents of those communities. As Emerson and Smith note in their book *Divided by Faith*, theological frameworks formed in isolation from diverse people groups can create behaviors that are diametrically opposed to stated beliefs (like believing in reconciliation while practicing homogeneity).[9] John Perkins has often described the typical white American evangelical Christian as a functional schizophrenic: someone who believes the Word of God but who won't do it. The Western church has grown out of step with mission.

Mission Values

Because I had been discipled in a foreign country, influenced by international leaders and missionaries, I found myself applying principles learned overseas to urban ministry in Denver. I moved into the city, making the urban community my home. Convinced that God was working either in (through the indwelling Spirit) or on (because God's desire is that all be saved) each of the people in my new neighborhood, I saw my task as being not only to share the gospel, but also to get close enough to local youth to discern God's activity and how to work in sync with it. Such convictions guided my actions, but in them I felt very alone. I was pioneering something I believed to be biblical, yet which seemed foreign to most ministry colleagues.

That is when I was introduced to John Perkins and his ministry philosophy.

John had already developed ministries in poor communities based on what he called the Three *R*s of Christian Community Development. These *R*s formed the core of his theological and missional rationale for working among the poor.

The longer we worked in the community of Mendenhall, the more God unfolded to us the real power of the Body, that it's not just a group. As Christians coming together, cemented by our central unifying commitment to Christ, we began to see how we could be transformed into corporate power, how we could corporately give our lives in the direction of evangelizing or economic development or relieving human need or justice and make a difference.

We must relearn what it means to be a body and what it means to continue Christ's ministry of preaching the gospel to the poor. I believe there is a strategy to do this. We have seen three principles work that seem to be at the heart of how a local body of Christians can affect their neighborhood. We call them the three "R's" of the quiet Revolution: *relocation*, *reconciliation*, and *redistribution*.[10]

I was thrilled to find someone whose ministry values seemed so closely aligned with the Scriptures, and whose philosophy and strategy were marked by integrity. The more I read John's books, the more I realized that he had taken mission principles—convictions dear to me—and pressed them into a ministry model that was effectively changing lives in urban communities. I was struck by the stature of his character: His hunger for God fueled his passion for justice for the poor; his humility made him both credible and approachable. In response to my need, God had brought into my life someone who would become for me a life-long mentor.

The core values of Christian Community Development (CCD) are also foundational to transformational discipleship. Early in our relationship, John expressed a burden that would shape my life's work. He asked: "How do we build incentive in inner-city youth? How can youth within broken families and communities be motivated toward Christ and a life of meaning and purpose? What will it take to do that?" I became convinced that the values of CCD would lead to answers to these questions.

So I took the guiding principles of CCD and treated them like a philosophical filter through which to examine youth and youth ministry. I pursued the question, "If I looked at youth ministry through the grid of CCD, what would it look like?"

Relocation

The initial intent of this value was to encourage youth indigenous to poor communities to get their college education and then re-turn—relocate—back into their home communities. Later the concept broadened to encourage Christians from a variety of back-grounds to make poor communities their home.

This principle has been called the "linchpin" of CCD. It is what sets the CCD philosophy of ministry apart from other urban min-istry approaches. It is also the value that has met with the greatest resistance. "God is not calling me to uproot my family and leave my safe community to serve the poor," many have responded. "I can serve them just as effectively from here. I don't have to live in their community."

In the face of this assertion, I recall Kelly and his brothers' re-sponse when I was robbed: "Now you understand. You are one of us now." As time went on, my "understanding" would extend far beyond what it felt like to be robbed. Why? I had incarnated myself into the community. True, I grew up in a neighborhood similar to theirs; I already knew firsthand the dynamics of growing up urban. Yet there were things I learned about their lives that I never would have known had I not relocated to their community.

More important, because I shared their community, *they* knew that *I* knew, which afforded me a level of credibility that those out-side the neighborhood did not possess.

As a kid, Charles attended some of our youth programs, but then he got caught up in gang life. A shooting left him paralyzed from the waist down. Later, when he was an adult, we reconnect-ed, and he shared something I never forgot: "Ted, you could talk to these guys [his gang member friends]. You know why? Because you're black and you're *here*."

Through the CCD grid, what does youth ministry look like? It looks like a ministry that emerges from within the community, because its leaders have made the community their home. Relocation—living among the poor as neighbors—positions the church to fulfill its purpose as salt and light for the world (see Matthew 5:13-16).

Reconciliation

The central focus of Christian ministry, and therefore of CCD, can be summed up in a single word: reconciliation. "All this is from God, who reconciled us to himself through Christ and gave us the ministry of reconciliation" (2 Corinthians 5:18). Dr. Wayne Gordon, chairman of the Christian Community Development Association, writes:

> Christian community development is concerned with reconciling people to God and bringing them into a church fellowship where they can be discipled in their faith. . . .
>
> Can a gospel that reconciles people to God without reconciling people to people be the true gospel of Jesus Christ? A person's love for Christ should break down every racial, ethnic and economic barrier in a united effort to solve the problems of the community. For example, Christian community development recognizes that the entire Body of Christ—black, white, brown and yellow; rich and poor; urban and suburban; educated and uneducated—needs to share the task of loving the poor.[11]

To be a reconciler is to be a peacemaker—and to be a peacemaker is to be "blessed. . . for they will be called children of God" (Matthew 5:9). A peacemaker is burdened by the enmity that exists between two entities that should be united. The task of the peacemaker is to facilitate reunion—to point fallen people toward the relationship they were created to have with the living God and with one another. We are like our Father, Jesus says, when we live as peacemakers. And we are "blessed"—happy, connected, Kingdom people—when we do so.

The principle of reconciliation plays out in youth ministry in two dynamic ways. It begins by engaging in what Francis Schaeffer called providing "honest answers to honest questions." Too often youth workers deny themselves the experience of directly applying God's truth to felt needs. We spend more time asserting than listening! Taking time to grasp and address barriers keeping youth from a relationship with God means two things: dealing with misconceptions about the Christian faith, and sharing the gospel in ways it can be understood (in bite-sized pieces).

It is when youth (and the adults ministering among them) honestly address these barriers that a second important dimension of a reconciliation ministry emerges. At some point, a young person will share among their peers something of an intimate nature. It could be in the form of a confession or some other personal revelation. The moment that happens, I yell: "Stop! Did you hear that? [Name] just shared something personal. This stays with us; it doesn't leave this room!!" This establishes the group as a safe place to be genuine and honest. It marks the first step toward *establishing the social context of engaging God together.* The group meeting becomes a place where reconciliation is actively pursued.

Through the CCD grid, what does youth ministry look like? It looks like a ministry engaged in peacemaking, and in sharing the good news of the gospel in ways that speak to young people's deepest needs and encourage mutual growth.

Redistribution

Redistribution… brings new skills, new relationships and new resources and puts them to work to empower the residents of a given community to bring about healthy transformation. This is redistribution: when Christian Community Development ministries harness the commitment and energy of men, women and young people living in the community, and others who care about their community, and find creative avenues to develop jobs, schools, health centers, home ownership opportunities and other enterprises of long-term development.[12]

In transformational discipleship, redistribution manifests itself primarily in the area of capacity discovery among youth, and in the unleashing of those capacities in ways that benefit children—the following generation. It is putting the resources of youth to work for the good of the community.

The discovery and unleashing of adolescent capacity is rare in youth ministry. Even those ministries that value capacity discovery often fall short of creating avenues through which youthful capacities can contribute in meaningful ways to the advancement of God's kingdom. A significant reason why there are few young Davids or Esthers or Josephs in our world today is that the church has organized itself around the false assumption that youth cannot lead. The result is leadership development programs that provide classroom-like instruction but little meaningful experience.

Similarly, genuine leadership opportunities for young people are rare in academic settings. I remember asking Skye, a high school leader, "How does what we do here in Neighborhood compare with the leadership instruction you're receiving at school?"

Her response was immediate and to the point: "There they talk about leadership. Here you do it."

I knew we were making a difference when children came to me asking, "Can I do what they [the emerging leaders] do someday?" The seeds of redistribution were sprouting in our ministry.

Peering through the CCD grid, what does youth ministry look like? It looks like a ministry engaged in redistribution: the unleashing and nurturing of capacity in ways that invest in the long-term development of youth and children.

Mission and Transformational Discipleship

John Perkins's Three *R*s were eventually expanded to become the Eight Key Components of Christian Community Development. The added five elements are significant outgrowths of the first three. As John has said, relocation is incarnation; the incarnation is both God's method and model of bringing salvation to a needy world. Redistribution leads to *leadership development* and *empowerment*. Reconciliation is a ministry given specifically to the church, hence the importance of *church-based* ministry. Such a ministry requires *listening* and applying the gospel to felt needs. This leads to a *wholistic* engagement with people.

God never intended His church to separate along racial or economic lines. Those lines do exist; homogeneity and class distinctions are realities in our world. But it was never God's intent that we follow after or shape our theology around such divisions. No, union with Christ means a counter-cultural existence. That existence is expressed in the eight key principles of CCD:

1. We show special concern for the marginalized around us, and position ourselves to serve them (relocation).
2. We live as people who acknowledge, as did Job, that the same God who made the poor made us (reconciliation).
3. We see ourselves as stewards of God's creation and treat possessions, both financial and human capital, as belonging to God (redistribution).
4. We pursue among all people, youth in particular, the maturing of God-given capacity (leadership development).
5. As with Jesus and the woman at the well, the felt needs of others become the context in which the good news of the gospel is shared (listening to the community).

6. We the church, God's people, are charged to make a difference in society (church-based).
7. As such, we position ourselves to touch every aspect of a person's life (wholistic approach).
8. In this way we empower people to be all God intended them to be (empowerment).[13]

Mission—participating in Christ's ongoing work as witnesses and pointers to His love for the sake of the world—is the driving force behind transformational discipleship. This is as it was meant to be. In an exciting way, the phenomenon of the world coming to the city has given the church another opportunity to get mission right.

Given the expanding reality of youth growing up urban, the recognition of mission as a driving force to reach the young and vulnerable in our cities is coming to us none too soon.

Notes
1. Ray Bakke, *A Theology as Big as the City* (Downers Grove, IL: InterVarsity Press, 1997), p. 34.
2. Rainer D. Riesner, "Galilee," in *Dictionary of Jesus and the Gospels*, eds. Joel B. Green, Scot McKnight and I. Howard Marshall (Downers Grove, IL: InterVarsity Press, 1992), pp. 252-253.
3. Bakke, *A Theology as Big as the City*, pp. 131-132.
4. David J. Bosch, *Transforming Mission: Paradigm Shifts in Theology of Mission* (Maryknoll, NY: Orbis Books, 1991).
5. Dr. Mary Klages, Postmodernism, http://www.bdavetian.com/Postmodernism.html, last revision: April 21, 2003, accessed March 2010.
6. Bosch, *Transforming Mission*, pp. 368-510.
7. Robert Lupton, *Compassion, Justice and the Christian Life: Rethinking Ministry to the Poor* (Ventura, CA: Regal Books, 2007), p. 128.
8. Bakke, *A Theology as Big as the City*, pp. 34-35.
9. Michael O. Emerson and Christian Smith, *Divided by Faith: Evangelical Religion and the Problem of Race in America* (Oxford: Oxford University Press, 2000).
10. John M. Perkins, *A Quiet Revolution: The Christian Response to Human Need, a Strategy for Today* (Waco, TX: Word Incorporated, 1976), pp. 217-218.
11. Dr. Wayne L. Gordon, "The Eight Components of Christian Community Development," in Robert Lupton, *Compassion, Justice and the Christian Life: Rethinking Ministry to the Poor* (Ventura, CA: Regal Books, 2007), pp. 126-127.
12. Ibid., p. 128.
13. Ibid., pp. 123-135.

Questions for Thought

1. Do you agree that mission is no longer an activity but an attribute of God characterizing the entire church? If so, how do you see this attribute reflected in your church?

2. If you were to make loving neighbor the umbrella context of your youth ministry, what would change?

3. In what ways does your ministry discover and unleash leadership capacity among youth? How can your ministry grow in empowering and equipping young people to lead?

Chapter 7

GROWING UP URBAN

THE POWER OF THE CODE

She cried all the way home.

Our weeklong summer youth camp in the mountains was over. What a difference a week makes! The van ride to camp had been loud and raucous—kids were excited beyond belief. Now, as we headed home, their demeanor was quiet and subdued. Some slept, while others watched as the mountains grew smaller in the distance. We were on our way back to the city. Overall, the mood was one of contentment.

Except for her. She sat in the very back, trying to go unnoticed. But the glistening tears on her face and the slight heaving of her shoulders revealed that she was sobbing. When I asked others about her, they said she was alright. No one seemed overly concerned. It was as if I were among family members of someone who had just lost a loved one. People around her knew she needed space to grieve.

As I pondered the situation, a Scripture passage came to mind. It was Jesus' final assessment of the man from whom an evil spirit had left—only to return with friends:

And the final condition of that person is worse than the first (Luke 11:26).

Had I, through this wonderful (albeit brief) camping experience, set the stage for despair? By exposing inner-city youth to the joys of summer camp, was I making their return to life in the 'hood even more painful?

Years later, I asked Paulette about that experience, and she recalled the moment this way:

> As you know, Ted . . . I didn't like coming home. There was the yellin', the arguin', the cursin', the fightin'. And when I was at camp, I didn't have none of that. I woke up to a peaceful voice: "[lyrically] It's time to get uh-up!" We'd wake to a bell or something . . .
>
> I felt safe at camp. I was around lovely people. I didn't hear no yellin', no cursin', no drinkin' alcohol: no, none of that. And it was exciting for me to go to camp and to come to club.

The sobbing girl in the back of the van was not shedding the tears of joy and gratitude that are common after an intense mountaintop experience. Rather, her tears were those of despair and hopelessness. They were the cries of an urban adolescent returning home.

Adolescence

The term "adolescence" comes from the Latin *adolescere,* which means "grow to maturity."[1] Until the late nineteenth century, adolescence was not singled out as a distinct stage of human development. But it was there. As far back as the fourth century BC, the Greek philosopher Aristotle observed:

> They [young people at this stage of life] are changeable and fickle in their desires, which are violent while they last, but quickly over: their impulses are keen but not deep-rooted.[2]

Aristotle's teacher, Plato, made similar remarks. Centuries later, in 1904, G. Stanley Hall would advance for the first time a definition of adolescence. Human development, Hall proposed, traveled through a series of stages, from primitive (childhood) to savage (adolescence) to mature (adulthood). Writing about Hall's characterization of adolescence, Rolf Muuss, in his work *Theories of Adolescence*, explains:

> He perceived the emotional life of the adolescent as an oscillation between contradictory tendencies. Energy, exaltation, and supernatural activity are followed by indifference, lethargy, and loathing. Exuberant gaiety, laughter, and euphoria make place for dysphoria, depressive gloom, and melancholy. Egoism, vanity, and conceit are just as characteristic of this period of life as are abasement, humiliation, and bashfulness. One can observe both the remnants of an uninhibited childish selfishness and increasing idealistic altruism. Goodness and virtue are never so pure, but never again does temptation so forcefully preoccupy thought.[3]

It is no accident that the recognition of this unique phase in life coincided with the rise of the American Industrial Revolution. As Larry Brentro and Scott Larson point out in their book *Reclaiming Our Prodigal Sons and Daughters: A Practical Approach for Connecting with Youth in Conflict,* America's shift from an agrarian to an industrial society brought adolescence out of the shadows into plain sight.

> Prior to the industrial revolution, it was necessary that everyone in the family, from age 5 up, work. . . . The transition from childhood to adulthood was relatively smooth, as young people were naturally apprenticed into the adult world of work and responsibility. But with the dawn of industrialization, modern society began segregating young people from the world of adults. . . . Beginning in 1890, scientists began formulating the concept of *adolescents.*[4]

Among the volumes of research on the nature of adolescence, one person's findings stand out as most definitive: Erik Erikson's theories on identity development.

Mankind, Erikson asserts, goes through stages of human development. Each stage is dominated by a developmental "crisis"—a life-shaping, character-defining issue. He calls these the Eight Stages of Man:

1. *Infancy: Trust versus Mistrust* (the crisis: whether one becomes a trusting or mistrusting person).

2. *Eighteen months to 3½ years: Autonomy versus Shame and Doubt* (the crisis: whether one becomes an autonomous, creative individual or a dependent, inhibited, self-doubting individual).

3. *3½ to 6 years: Initiative versus Guilt* (the crisis: whether the child engages life with activity, curiosity and exploration, or experiences immobilization by fear and guilt).

4. *Pre-adolescence: Industry versus Inferiority* (the crisis: whether one develops a sense of industry or feelings of inferiority).

5. *Adolescence: Identity versus Identity Confusion* (the crisis: the extent to which one establishes a sense of personal identity and avoids role diffusion and identity confusion).

6. *Post-adolescence: Intimacy versus Isolation* (the crisis: whether one finds either intimacy or isolation in interpersonal relationships).

7. *Adult life: Generativity versus Stagnation* (the crisis: whether one experiences productive creativity in terms of vocational contribution to society, or stagnation marked by egotism, self-absorption and self-indulgence).

8. *Old age: Integrity versus Despair* (the crisis: the final stage in the human life cycle, where the developmental challenge is achievement of ego-integrity versus disgust and despair).[5]

Each stage in life has a dominant life issue. The crisis of identity can indeed surface during other stages in life (in fact, some may struggle with it throughout their lives), but it is most prominent during the time of adolescence. Adolescents are wired to seek answers to identity questions: "Where did I come from?" "Who am I?" "What will I become?" The search for identity is, for the adolescent, a key driver and motivational issue.

Urban Adolescence

Urban youth must navigate the already stressful adolescent experience within the pressurized context of a ghetto environment.

Early in their teen years, urban youth are dealing with challenges most middle-class American adults have never had to face. One day a school social worker asked me to meet with her. When I arrived at her office, she said, "I told E— I was meeting with you today. He asked me to show you these." She handed me a stack of about 20 test papers and homework assignments. They were graded: one *B* and the rest *A*s. She explained: "He's proud of these. His grades seemed to improve around the time he joined your program." (This was interesting, since at the time we had no educational component, only the weekly club gathering.) "But they've dropped recently. Do you know why? Has something changed?"

Something had changed—twice. First, after years of living in the Five Points projects, E— and his family had moved to an adjacent neighborhood. For a single mother raising young boys, distancing her family from the gang and drug activity dominating the projects was like escaping a war zone. But she had struggled with rent payments. What the social worker had witnessed were the ripple effects of trauma surrounding the second change: About a month before our meeting, E—'s family had been forced to move back into the projects.

On another occasion, two of our youth group members—Marvin and Anthony—did not come to club. I later learned they had gotten into a fight. Marvin, as he was prone to do, lost control (he "lost it," the kids said) and found a brick. Next thing they knew, Anthony was lying on the ground in a pool of his own blood.

One night after club, Glen confronted me. "Jesus may be fine for you, but I'm not turning out any different from my stepdad." Glen's stepdad had taught his boys how to steal. He would take them to a store and say, "Steal all you can. If you get caught, don't worry. I'll bail you out and tell them I'll beat you when I get you home."

Author and poet Useni Eugene Perkins describes a summer experience in what he calls the "ghetcolony of the city." Speaking not only as a sociologist but also as someone who grew up in the Bronzeville community on Chicago's south side, Perkins captures an arresting snapshot of city life:

> Summer mornings never appear to change. They quickly become a part of ghetcolony tradition, a pervasive episode of hopelessness and poverty. What was true yesterday is more than likely to be true today. . . .
>
> On hot days one can see fatigued ebony faces protruding out of windows to gain relief from the morning humidity. And the stenchy alleys covered with broken wine bottles, empty beer cans, urine, and the feces of stray dogs and unwanted people. And the weary people waiting on street corners to catch the crowded buses which take them to work. And the school aged children who leave home before they have eaten breakfast. And the whimpers of babies who are still hungry from yesterday's shortage of milk. And the dispossessed men who mill in front of taverns waiting to quench their hunger with anything that can help them escape their pain and frustration. And the hustlers, pimps, street men and other social outcasts who serve as models for the young.[6]

Contrary to the media's obsession with the violent nature of the city, there is a richness to urban life that is rarely displayed on the big screen. It can be found in relationships, shared history, and the resilience of the human spirit. One of the cable television networks touts as its slogan "Characters welcome." This could just as easily be the slogan for many an urban community. I am constantly amazed at the creative and fascinating characters that reside in the city, particularly among its young. There are wonderful people living here. Sharing life as neighbors has brought great joy to my family over the years.

Yet passersby who observe children playing on the streets of the asphalt jungle and conclude, "They are happy; there is nothing wrong," are perhaps guilty of seeking justification for indifference. There are many things wrong, and those who grow up urban, despite moments of reprieve or celebration, are highly vulnerable to the influence of the streets.

Code of the Streets

Useni Perkins describes this unique aspect of growing up urban, which, in my estimation, poses the greatest challenge to urban youth ministry:

> And it is on the streets where the Black child receives his basic orientation to life. The streets become his primary reference. . . . For a child to survive the "ghetcolony" he must undergo a rigorous apprenticeship. . . . He becomes a student of the "asphalt jungle."[7]

The black child's worldview—his/her understanding of how life works—is indelibly shaped by a culture dominated by violence, crime, instability and fear. This is true for all who grow up urban. The "ghetcolony" is more than an experience. It is an orientation. Elijah Anderson, in his signature book by the same name, refers to it as the Code of the Street:

> Although there are often forces in the community that can counteract negative influences—by far the most powerful

is a strong, loving, "decent" (as inner-city residents put it) family that is committed to middle class values—*the despair is pervasive enough to have spawned an oppositional culture, that of "the street,"* whose norms are often consciously opposed to those of mainstream society. . . .

The street culture has evolved a "code of the street," which amounts to *a set of informal rules governing interpersonal public behavior, particularly violence.*[8] (emphasis added)

Anderson's description of urban life is vivid and powerful. The city is filled with all kinds of people: "street" kids and "decent" kids, working parents and gang members, faithful grandmothers, single moms, drug dealers, prostitutes, and the like. What boggles the mind is the extent to which all are impacted by the code of the street. The code has an identity-shaping influence on the lives of every person in the urban community.

In his review of Anderson's book, researcher and educational policy expert Kevin R. Kosar describes the phenomenon in this way:

One might wonder just how this self-destructive environment perpetuates itself. . . .

Anderson explains that the ghetto regenerates itself through "the code of the street." The code is a hierarchy of values that exalts impudence, machismo, and regular displays of violence while it denigrates manners, responsibility, and compassion. Children born in or brought to the inner-city face the inescapable "dilemma of the decent child"; either be a good kid like your parents and teachers tell you and get beat up by other kids, or start behaving like a thug or "gangsta." Understandably, a great many youths choose the latter path. Thus the "hood" lives on, transcending individuals and sucking in more and more children into criminal behavior, despite the best efforts of some parents.[9]

Much has been written about the dynamics of city life and urban culture's impact on its residents. The influence of the code is far more pervasive than one might think. It creates a mindset—a value system—that, for many, shapes destinies.

For years I led a weekly Bible study with men transitioning out of incarceration and/or drug addiction. Some were in their twenties, while many were in their forties and fifties. In ways similar to a youth setting, I confronted belief systems and values born out of the culture of the streets. At the heart of the Bible study was a competing for minds—urging the replacement of street paradigms with kingdom-of-God values.

Among its many tenets, the code has a way of defining race. What does it mean to be black? By what standard is "blackness" measured? For many young blacks in urban America, to resist the code is to deny one's racial identity. Embracing the rules of the street gives credence to your racial affiliation: you're "acting black." Resistance—choosing to be a good kid, get good grades, etc.—signals a denial of race: you're "acting white." This creates an unresolvable dilemma if one accepts the premise that identity is determined by response to the cultural mores of the day.

I think back to my friend at the church missions conference who could not bring himself to co-teach the class on urban mission (see chapter 4, "Tapestry"). His response seemed irrational: "My neighborhood was terrible.... I'll never go back.... I'm not going in there [the classroom!]." Then I realized: Of course it's irrational! It is part of the identity struggle. I know blacks for whom the thought of returning to the city evokes great fear, as if some negative force might engulf them.

Urban Politique

Politics has a way of seeping into every social dilemma. Most analysts cannot talk about city problems without injecting politicized opinions as to why they exist—or proposing solutions that favor a particular political agenda.

This is clearly expressed in Elijah Anderson's and Eugene Perkins' assessments of urban issues:

> The inclination to violence springs from the circumstances of life among the ghetto poor—the lack of jobs that pay a living wage, limited basic public services (police response in emergencies, building maintenance, trash pickup, lighting, and other services that middle-class neighborhoods take for granted), the stigma of race, the fallout from rampant drug use and drug trafficking, and the resulting alienation and absence of hope for the future.[10] (Anderson)

> The streets become his primary reference because other institutions have failed to provide him with the essential skills he needs to survive in the "ghetcolony".[11] (Perkins)

Toward the end of his book, Anderson highlights what he deems an important solution: provide jobs with a living wage. When compared to the depth of the urban challenge, a response like this seems anemic, almost laughable. Good economic policy is important, but applied in isolation it hardly scratches the surface of addressing the influence of the code on the young.

Charles Lipson, a professor of political science at the University of Chicago, wrote an article on the violence that took place in Chicago over the 2014 Independence Day weekend. Eighty-two people were shot; 17 died. Most of the victims were in their late teens and twenties. "Who knows how many innocents were hit by stray bullets or huddled under their beds for protection?" he asks. "How many children think gunfire is a normal background noise?"

Later in the article, Lipson touches on the failure of public policy and the need for more grassroots solutions:

> We have not ignored the fundamental social problems that lie behind this cycle of violence, poverty and family

disintegration. We have tried hard to address them, but we've failed. Over the past 50 years, we have poured trillions of dollars into Great Society programs that experts said would alleviate poverty, strengthen families, build job skills and reduce crime. These costly programs were dreamed up in Washington, passed by well-meaning legislators and administered by increasingly powerful bureaucrats. The programs haven't just failed, they often have made the problems worse. The catastrophic rise of out-of wedlock births and the collapse of nuclear families have gone hand-in-hand with those "helpful" programs. What the laws, regulations and subsidies did was create dependency, encourage single parenthood and *undermine the private institutions that once buttressed communities.*

We are now reaping the whirlwind. It's time to begin fundamentally rethinking how we spend money for schools, social services and police. *We should begin by scaling back the dead hand of Washington and encouraging more local experimentation.*[12] (emphasis added)

A significant private institution that has been undermined is the local church and its youth ministry. Sadly, it is an undermining of our own choosing. How have we allowed this to happen? *By allowing highly politicized socio-political perspectives on the urban youth crisis to overshadow Christian perspectives and resources.*

As I consider the current state of the American inner city, two illustrations come to mind. A defining story within Star Trek lore is how James Kirk beat the Kobayashi Maru—an impossible-to-win Starfleet exercise designed to test the character of cadets training for command positions. In effect, Kirk cheated: He changed the conditions of the test, declaring, "I don't believe in the no-win scenario." Trekkies understand this to mean that discovering a solution often requires redefining the problem.

A second illustration comes from Bobb Biehl's Masterplanning Arrow—a tool used to map the direction of an organization. A preparatory step in the goal-setting process is identifying your top three roadblocks and top three resources. Leadership requires an awareness of both, to the end of utilizing one's resources to overcome roadblocks.

If the solutions to today's urban issues lie solely within the realms of the political and the socioeconomic, then what can a lowly youth worker accomplish? Likely very little. But if there are spiritual and relational aspects to the situation, then there are resources uniquely available to the Christian leader that have been overshadowed and underutilized. As with the Kobayashi Maru, achieving success in this arena requires redefining the problem.

I remember distinctly my first Christmas after giving my life to Christ. I had already made plans to fly home for two weeks. Fear of returning to my home environment gripped me. I was terrified to go back, for fear I would somehow lose this "feeling" of new life within me. With great anxiety, I shared my dilemma with the man who had led me to Christ.

I tried as best I could to describe the source of my fears—the harsh realities of my neighborhood. As I talked, I noticed Bud smiling. I thought to myself, *He's not understanding what I'm saying.* So I continued, adding graphic detail to the description of my city. But the more I talked, the bigger he smiled.

Finally, in vintage Bud fashion, he burst out in a hearty laugh. Then, in a strangely reflective yet joyful tone, he said, "What a tremendous opportunity!"

I thought he was crazy.

In actuality, he was right. I survived my stay at home. I even made new Christian friends who introduced me to a wonderful local church body. When I returned to Vienna after the holidays, I made a plaque and hung it on my wall. It read, in big bright letters: "What a Tremendous Opportunity!"

So much focus is given to the pragmatic nature of problems, we fail to look for (or recognize) divine solutions. We miss the "Tremendous Opportunity." It is time to look at the urban community from another perspective. We must answer the strategic question, Where is God in all of this?

Notes

1. *New Oxford American Dictionary*, Third Edition (New York: Oxford University Press, 2010).
2. Rolf E. Muuss, *Theories of Adolescence* (New York: McGraw-Hill, 1996), p. 5.
3. Ibid., p. 16.
4. Scott Larson and Larry Brendtro, *Reclaiming Our Prodigal Sons and Daughters: A Practical Approach for Connecting with Youth in Conflict* (Bloomington, IN: Solution Tree, 2000), p. 4.
5. Muuss, *Theories of Adolescence*, pp. 47-57.
6. Quoted in Jawanza Kunjufu, *Countering the Conspiracy to Destroy Black Boys* (Sauk Village, IL: African American Images, 1985), pp. 16-17.
7. Ibid., p. 17.
8. Elijah Anderson, *Code of the Street: Decency, Violence, and the Moral Life of the Inner City* (New York: W. W. Norton & Company, 1999), Kindle edition.
9. Kevin R. Kosar, "The Underclass Up Close," in *The Wagner Review* (New York: Robert F. Wagner Graduate School of Public Service, Spring 2000), p. 141.
10. Anderson, *Code of the Street*.
11. Kunjufu, *Countering the Conspiracy to Destroy Black Boys*, p. 17.
12. Charles Lipson, "Summer Weekend 2014 Worse than St. Valentine's Day Massacre," in *The Chicago Tribune*, July 10, 2014.

Questions for Thought

1. In what ways do you see the code of the streets affecting the behavior of people in your neighborhood? Families? Kids? Your church? You?

2. In relation to coping with life in the 'hood, what do you hear youth saying are their greatest felt needs?

3. Describe the Kobayashi Marus (i.e., the seemingly impossible situations) you and your ministry face as a result of the code of the street.

Chapter 8

THE DIVINE IMPRINT

"AND GOD MADE MANKIND IN HIS IMAGE . . ."

There can be no doubt about it: Children are special in the kingdom of God.

> People were bringing little children to Jesus for him to place his hands on them, but the disciples rebuked them. When Jesus saw this, he was indignant. He said to them, "Let the little children come to me, and do not hinder them, for the kingdom of God belongs to such as these. Truly I tell you, anyone who will not receive the kingdom of God like a little child will never enter it." And he took the children in his arms, placed his hands on them and blessed them (Mark 10:13-16).

For followers of Jesus, though they may have struggled to understand at first, stories and sayings about children became important and instructive. The child was a metaphor for discipleship and Kingdom character. Divine power, Jesus asserts, emerges from weakness; true greatness lies in becoming least of all for Jesus' sake (see Mark 10:41-45). The phrases "such as these" and "like a little child" point to the childlike character necessary for entrance into the kingdom of God.

Passages like these also draw attention to the esteemed position children hold within Christendom. One commentator writes: "Jesus was one of the first ever to see how essentially precious any person is, particularly a young child. A concern for children was not invented by the welfare state: it goes back to the teaching of Jesus."[1]

In the previous chapter, we explored the challenges of growing up urban. Youth residing in inner-city communities are labeled "at-risk" because of the surrounding dangers and pressures to conform to destructive patterns of behavior in order to survive. It can be argued that all children are at-risk simply because they are children. Their fate lies outside their control—with adults who may or may not care for them, and a broader society that may or may not protect them.

Now let's consider the Greek society of Jesus' day, in which children were treated as property to be kept or discarded at a father's discretion:

> An infant could be abandoned without penalty or social stigma for many reasons, including an anomalous appearance, being an illegitimate child or grandchild or a child of infidelity, family poverty, parental conflict. . . or being one of too many children. Sometimes [they] were given to friends, but more often than not they were abandoned to the elements, and death resulted from hypoglycemia and hypothermia. Sometimes the infant was devoured by the dogs that scavenged public places. It was likely, however, that [they] were rescued from these fates and picked up by slavers. Abandonment generally occurred in a public place, where it was hoped that the infant could be taken up by some wealthy person.
>
> If picked up by wealthy persons, the child could become a slave, a play companion for another child, a pet, or a prostitute; it could be sold for begging purposes after mutilation or become a truly adopted child, a treasured alumnus.[2]

While modern Western societies generally value children, to-day's urban child has been "abandoned" to the code of the street. For these children, despair and hopelessness show up at a young age. Education specialist Jawanza Kunjufu describes what he calls the Fourth Grade Failure Syndrome: By the time black boys reach the fourth grade, their natural excitement about life fades into a lethargic sense of hopelessness.[3] Children are highly perceptive. It was an arresting moment when a five-year-old boy said to his father: "Dad, do I have to be black? It's better to be white."

"How do we build incentive in inner-city youth? How can youth within broken families and communities be motivated toward Christ and a life of meaning and purpose? What will it take to do that?" The question John Perkins posed years ago still cries out for answers. What is the Christian response to the conforming power and identity-shaping influence of the ghetto?

"In the beginning . . ."—before there were ghettos and street codes—". *. . God created the heavens and the earth."* Could it be that God has already spoken on this subject? At first glance, Genesis 1:1 seems too simplistic a response to an issue of such magnitude as the controlling influence of ghetto life. And yet, treated seriously, the impact of creation on motivating at-risk youth is significant.

The realities of creation gradually informed my response to John Perkins's question and brought a new perspective to the urban challenge. The conditions of the Kobayashi Maru had changed.

This did not happen overnight. Many assisted in my journey toward discovery. One of my guides was Maria Montessori.

The Absorbent Mind

"The child is endowed with unknown powers, which can guide [mankind] to a radiant future."[4] This was a core belief of Maria Montessori, founder of the educational method that bears her name.

Montessori believed that children are born with the drive and capacity to absorb the culture surrounding them. The book titled

The Absorbent Mind is a compilation of Montessori's lectures describing her education model.

> Ours was a house for children, rather than a real school. We had prepared a place for children where a diffused culture could be assimilated from the environment, without any need for direct instruction. The children who came were from the humblest social levels, and their parents were illiterate. Yet these children learned to read and write before they were five, and no one had given them any lessons. If visitors asked them, "Who taught you to write?" they often answered with astonishment: "Taught me? No one has taught me!"[5]

Parents often take credit for teaching their children to walk and talk. From Montessori's perspective, parents do not teach— they *guide*. Children do not need convincing; they are relentlessly motivated to walk and talk. They were created that way!

Montessori studied philosophy and psychology, graduating from Rome University medical school as the first female Italian physician in 1896. Five years later, she became director of a small school for "challenged" youth. She insisted that her staff recognize each patient's need for stimulation, purposeful activity and self-esteem. She became convinced that children were capable of sustained concentration; they enjoyed order and preferred work to play. She went on to design a program that taught young children how to care for themselves and their environment. Her methods were experimental, but they produced seemingly miraculous results.

In 1907, Montessori opened a day care center, the Casa dei Bambini (Children's House), where she applied her theories and methods of child education. The Casa dei Bambini's students came from the slums of Rome and were generally described as disadvantaged.

The original Children's House and those that followed were designed to provide a stimulating environment for children to live, learn, and take responsibility for themselves. An emphasis was placed on self-determination and self-realization. This entailed developing a concern for others and discipline; to do this, children engaged in exercises in daily living. These and other exercises were to function like a ladder—allowing children to pick up the challenge and to judge their progress. "The essential thing is for the task to arouse such an interest that it engages the child's whole personality."[6]

Children entering Montessori's program were deemed "wild and unruly." Yet they responded to her teaching methods. Amazing things began to happen. Children younger than three years of age would "absorb" not just reading and writing, but also subjects like botany, zoology, mathematics and geography. They did this naturally, spontaneously and tirelessly.

The child's innate capacity to absorb knowledge, Montessori deduced, is fueled by a natural drive toward independence, as evidenced by children's incessant questioning and their inability to stop talking once they start. This impacts the role of the adult educator. The child—the absorbent mind—requires an environment conducive to discovery and growth. This, Montessori asserts, is true for all children, including the "deviated" child, whose natural desire for work and discovery has been corrupted.

> The environment must be rich in motives which lend interest to activity and invite the child to conduct his own experiences. These are principles dictated by life and by nature, which help the deviated child who has acquired regressive characteristics, to pass from the tendency to laziness to the desire for work, from lethargy and inertia to activity, from a state of fear (which shows itself sometimes in excessive attachment to people from whom the child cannot be separated) to a joyous freedom, the freedom to begin the conquest of life.

From inertia to work! This is the path of cure, just
as it is the path of development for the normal child.[7]

I was first exposed to the Montessori method when our local
elementary school (the school my children would later attend)
became a Montessori magnet school. The classroom was fascinating to watch: children moving freely among various activity
stations, focused on learning, listening intently to their teacher,
highly self-motivated.

Montessori, I discovered, had been fascinated by the intrica-
cies of creation. While acknowledging the evolutionary nature
of embryonic development, she noted innate learning capacities
unique to mankind. Her language at times sounded New Age
(e.g., her use of the phrase "psychic power"), yet her ideas flowed
out of a Judeo-Christian framework.

Dr. Scottie May, Assistant Professor of Christian Formation
and Ministry at Wheaton College, affirms this:

> As a young practitioner, Montessori was essentially a
> freethinker, especially when it came to the doctrines of
> the church. Mario Montessori (her son) gave a series of
> lectures in London in 1961 in which he described part
> of her spiritual journey: The more Maria worked with
> children, the more she saw the creative presence of God
> within them. A subtitle of a chapter in *The Child in the
> Church* (Montessori, 1965, 4) reads, "God Created The
> Child More Admirable Than We Think."[8]

Montessori had discovered a link between creation and
motivation. That discovery birthed a new approach to child education. "What am I looking at?" I asked while observing the
Montessori method in action. "Is there something here that can
help me understand how to motivate urban youth?"

Clues

I was a journeyman in search of an undiscovered country. *What is the key to motivating inner-city youth?* Montessori had presented a clue—one I struggled to understand. *Where is God in this picture? What needs to be understood about human behavior? What can cause youth without hope to hope again?*

Over the years, I listened and observed and tried to connect dots. As in the Montessori classroom, clues were right in front of me, embodied in the behaviors and responses of the kids in our ministry. Gradually I learned how to "read" them. Interviews with now-adult alums of Neighborhood Ministries highlight the discoveries that took place over time.

Consider these reflections from a young man named Glen:

In the community, we'd go off from house to house, to Kenny's, Harold's. . . and their parents would be like our parents: "Yeah, get on, get on . . ." [They] wasn't willing to listen. We had something to say! But it was foolish to the adult ears. . . . Now your presence on the scene, as an adult, showed me that if you're willing to spend time with us, and not run us off. . . willin' to communicate with us, let us have our freedom? That was a big plus for us.

I mean, takin' a chance, comin' into the neighborhood? You was a straight stranger, Ted, even as a black man! I mean, when you hit 34th Avenue, and came down into the Black Hole. . . an adult, taking time for us? Something our parents wouldn't do?

And the fact that you'd get us and take us out. . . . We knew what to look forward to when you brought us back. But the fact that you'd give us that time out. . . and everybody needs a time out. That's what you brought to the table.

Glen was a "founding member" of Neighborhood Ministries. My work with Youth for Christ involved getting referrals from juvenile probation. One of those referrals was Kelly, Glen's older brother. You may recall my mentioning Kelly before—he was the one who exercised his leadership potential by being the best thief on the block. "Hey, Ted, can I invite some friends to join us?" Kelly asked one day. Overnight a boys club was formed, and Glen was part of that fledgling group.

In those days I had two agendas. One was to do my job—to fulfill my responsibilities as a staff member of a Christian organization. But I also looked beyond the status quo, searching for more effective ways to reach urban youth. One of my first discoveries was that youth need a safe space—a place where they can be real without fear of retaliation or judgment.

I grew up in a neighborhood similar to Glen's, but I was never a "street" kid. Like all urban youth, I learned to threat-assess, but beyond that I was not street-wise. Imagine my embarrassment when Glen shared how my naiveté had turned into something good:

> There was a lot of kids we went to school with [there was bussing at the time] who lived on the other side of Colorado Boulevard. That was like a no-no for us; we roamed around the Cole neighborhood, but the other side of Colorado Boulevard—that was *their* territory.
>
> So when you'd gather us up, and we'd travel 'cross Colorado Boulevard [beginning to laugh] we'd do this [ducking down]! We knew you didn't know! [laughter]. . . Yeah, we'd "scooch" down!. . . What happened was, once they realized who we was. . . we [declared] a truce. When we saw each other in school, it was on then. But at club? There was something about your ministry that penetrated the minds of the youngsters—the children of the neighborhood—that made us want to "cease fire."

Here I was, putting lives in danger, and did not know it! Yet something wonderful had happened. Rival youth had discovered a place not bound by gang or neighborhood codes of behavior. In club they could be themselves, ask any question, and discuss things they would not dare talk about anywhere else. That freedom was worth declaring a "cease fire."

I did not know about the ministry-related truce at the time. I only sensed the freedom of the young people in our group. Club was a place filled with the free exchange of ideas. That established an openness that traveled both ways: eagerness to speak and willingness to listen. Club grew into an ideal setting in which to talk about the good news of God in Jesus Christ, and to address misconceptions regarding the Christian faith.

This was an important piece to motivating urban youth. It was a clue.

Then there was Jimmy. In response to his serious interest in Christian ministry, I brought him on staff. Soon he took charge of the middle and high school clubs. Here's how he recalls that experience:

> I remember [when] you handed things off to me. It was exciting, and it was scary, but it was exciting because, to me, it was a sign of trust; it was also a sign of growth, which, in the 'hood, there was very little of that. People didn't trust who you are a lot, and people weren't really willing to give you a chance to grow, because you had already been labeled. So, because of that, people usually wrote you off....
>
> My time with Neighborhood. . . did not just prepare me for ministry; it prepared me for life. A lot of the lessons that were learned there. . . the life examples that was modeled by many people. . . I look back on how much of life has been affected by the people we dealt with. . . . I learned a lot of valuable lessons that helped me not only in my ministry life but in my personal life.

Through Jimmy, I began to connect expressions of personal desire with God's design. Jimmy's heartfelt desire was to work with kids. Where was that coming from, and how was I to respond? My role as his mentor gave me significant influence over the direction of his life. Had I ignored his desires, or taken advantage of his skills without concern for his future, he might have advanced through other means. But God had placed him into my care. What was I to do?

"Whoever is under a leader's direction should be under his protection."[9] In matters of urban discipleship, a leader's first responsibility is to his young emerging leaders and their growth and development. There was more to Jimmy than his "label." Beneath his street savviness lay deeper aptitudes, the source of which was tied to creation—the work of God.

The psalmist says: "Take delight in the LORD, and he will give you the desires of your heart" (Psalm 37:4). Jimmy was delighting in the Lord. His desire to influence kids motivated him to serve and grow. This was another clue.

And then there was Raquel:

Neighborhood gave me a place to feel safe; it was the one place I could go to where I knew I'd be in a healthy environment, around healthy people. I think that Neighborhood allowed me to let down my guard, when I knew that I couldn't do that just hanging out in the neighborhood, or even hanging out at home. . . . [Outside Neighborhood] I was never comfortable being "Raquel"; you always had to be a tough person who is ready to fight for whatever, for whatever reason. I knew that I didn't have to do that at Neighborhood. I felt safe. . . . There were people around me willing to be patient and help me learn, and even patient through that process [of learning] with me. . . .

Just hearing people say that you can do this, "I see it in you." I mean it goes a long way. . . . I didn't think those things about myself. . . . I'd always think of the kids who did work at Summer Program and think, "Oh, I don't think I have the skill or the capacity or the personality or whatever it takes," something like that.

But after being here, being around it for a while, after becoming a Christian and being more committed to my walk with Christ. . . that, in and of itself, was a huge transformation that happened within me.

We had known Raquel since she was seven years old. Her mother was one of the first members of the Mothers of Pre-Schoolers (MOPS) chapter Shelly had started years before. We had walked with her mom through the nightmare of a violent and dysfunctional marriage. The effects on Raquel were devastating. With her older brother engulfed in gang life, Raquel took on the role of surrogate mom to her younger siblings. During this time, she experienced the horrors of child abuse and a brutal stabbing. By the age of 16, she was a recluse—a school dropout who would not leave home except when accompanied by her mother.

At Shelly's urging, Raquel took a job with Neighborhood Ministries as a receptionist. Over time, she branched out into other ministry areas. She coordinated children's programs and assisted with middle and high school activities. At 19, as mentioned earlier, she directed the summer day camp and was instrumental in forming the Emerging Leaders Initiative, Neighborhood's high school leadership program.

Raquel responded to safety and a nurturing environment. She experienced the freedom to be "Raquel." She also drank in the opportunity to grow into her true self. The more at home she became with her identity (who God had made her to be), the stronger she grew.

Raquel completed her GED and finished college. Today she is a successful events planner for a major firm. Jimmy continues to work with kids in the Denver area, and Glen serves as a local pastor.

There are others with similar stories—young people who responded to the safe and nurturing environment Neighborhood Ministries provided. As we observed them growing and flourishing, we began to figure out where God was in the motivation question. *"In the beginning . . ."*—before youth were ignored or labeled or pressed by the code of the street—*". . . God created the heavens and the earth."*

What is the secret to motivating urban youth? Tapping into their divine imprint—the image of God.

God's Creation

The historical narrative of Genesis 1-2 represents the beginning of the earliest accounts of salvation history; it provides insight into the nature of God and His creation in general, and the purpose of man as set apart from the rest of creation in particular.

Key phrases inform our understanding of the text. The introductory verse (1:1) clearly introduces God as starting point: the central figure in history and the author of creation. What follows is a day-by-day accounting of God's creative activity, with each day's work being framed by the phrases "and God said" and "there was evening, and there was morning" (1:2-23). With each creative act, God sees, reasons, evaluates and measures ("And God saw that it was good" [vv. 10, 12, 18, 21, 25]).

On the sixth day, the language abruptly changes as the focus shifts to creating mankind (1:26). With all else, God simply declares; with man, He deliberates with Himself ("Let us make mankind in our image"). Man is set apart as a unique image-bearer and responsible caretaker for the rest of creation; they (man and woman) are blessed (endowed with favor) to fill and rule the earth (see 1:28). The remainder of the narrative segment (2:4b-22) provides a more detailed description of man's creation. Mankind becomes God's primary object; creation now serves as a setting in which God interacts with humanity. The theological center of the passage is Genesis 1:27—the declaration of man as image-bearer of God:

> So God created mankind in his own image,
> in the image of God he created them;
> male and female he created them.

For Job, sharing God's image was a defining and motivational key to righteous interaction with others.

> Whoever heard me spoke well of me,
> and those who saw me commended me,
> because I rescued the poor who cried for help,
> and the fatherless who had none to assist them.
> The one who was dying blessed me;
> I made the widow's heart sing.
> I put on righteousness as my clothing;
> justice was my robe and my turban.
> I was eyes to the blind
> and feet to the lame.
> I was a father to the needy;
> I took up the case of the stranger.
> I broke the fangs of the wicked
> and snatched the victims from their teeth (Job 29:11-17).

> If I have denied justice to any of my servants,
> whether male or female,
> when they had a grievance against me,
> what will I do when God confronts me?
> What will I answer when called to account?
> Did not he who made me in the womb make them?
> Did not the same one form us both within our mothers?
> (Job 31:13-15).

Marveling at God's creation is a privilege Christian doctors, scientists and educators have enjoyed, as did the psalmist long ago:

> For you created my inmost being;
>> you knit me together in my mother's womb.
> I praise you because I am fearfully and wonderfully made;
>> your works are wonderful,
>> I know that full well.
> My frame was not hidden from you
>> when I was made in the secret place,
>> when I was woven together in the depths of the earth.
> Your eyes saw my unformed body (Psalm 139:13-16a).

At one time, Christians embraced "worm theology," believing that self-abasement was necessary to receive divine mercy. A focus on the depravity of humanity and phrases like "but I am a worm and not a man" (Psalm 22:6) fed this perspective. It was reflected, so it was perceived, in Isaac Watts's hymn, "Alas! And Did My Savior Bleed," which asked the question, "Would He devote that sacred head for such a worm as I?"[10]

While worm theology no longer dominates the shaping of Christian identity and practice, neither—sadly—does the *imago Dei*. At a time when at-risk youth struggle to define themselves and to recognize their inherent value, Tom Skinner's take on Psalm 139:13-16 should resound throughout the urban community: "You are the crowning achievement of God's creation; there is no one in heaven or earth like you!"

The Image of God

What exactly is the image of God? The image of God distinguishes mankind from all other animals and manifests the family resemblance to our Creator and heavenly Father. While some may

use the terms "image" and "likeness" to refer to different categories, they both emphasize and clarify this same central idea.

According to author and apologist Peter May, the image of
God is seen in six distinctive characteristics of humanity:

1. *Creative.* Mankind reflects the creative capacity of God.
   Human creativity is of a different order, as mankind
   lacks God's power, intelligence and artistry. But mankind is capable of original and creative ideas.
2. *Intelligent.* The mind of God that lies behind the creation is reflected, albeit in very small measure, in
   mankind's capacity for understanding and rational
   thought. Man is capable, unlike the animals, of pondering the meaning of existence, the significance of actions and the prospects of destiny. As May notes: "The
   extraordinary Mind behind the Universe has given us
   minds to inquire, to reason and, as Kepler put it, 'to
   think God's thoughts after him.'"
3. *Aesthetic.* God is not only a great artist who has fashioned a beautiful creation, but He has also given mankind the capacity to appreciate great beauty.
4. *Moral.* While animals may suffer from fear, they have no
   natural sense of guilt or awareness of good and evil. Yet
   the human conscience is a major aspect of humanity.
   Paul's description of the internal dilemma of battling
   good and evil (see Romans 7) is a distinctive human
   phenomenon. Mankind wrestles with moral choices.
5. *Relational.* One has only to read novels or watch soap
   operas to realize that the dominant theme of human
   existence is relationships. Life, in a word, is about
   love. Mankind struggles to understand the source
   and meaning of love, which can only be found in God
   through Christ.
6. *Spiritual.* Mankind is incurably religious.

The power of imagery is in what it reflects. Images may be hazy or clear, distorted or accurate, but whatever their attributes, they do not exist on their own. Beyond the image lies a reality—in this case the reality of God. As May notes, the image of God in mankind not only helps self-perception, but it also reveals God to us.[11]

Much can be gleaned from the condensed yet excellent treatise on the image of God in an article by the biblical scholar Charles Lee Feinberg. Of all the relevant passages, Feinberg asserts, the Genesis account is key. Feinberg raises three questions: (1) Of what specifically does the image of God consist? (2) What effect did sin and the fall of man have on this image? (3) What effect does the redemptive work of Christ have on the image of God?

May's observations address the first question. In Genesis 1:26, we find that man is the apex of all creation, possesses a special nature far superior to and never duplicated in lower animals, and is distinctive in his dominion over the rest of creation.

As to the second question, Feinberg notes that nowhere does the Bible indicate that divine image and likeness are lost due to sin. Man's nature still reflects the work and creation of God (see Deut. 32:6; Isa. 45:11; 54:5; 64:8; Acts 17:25; Rev. 4:11; Job 10:8-12; Ps. 139:14-16). Fallen man is still man; while marred, corrupted and in an impaired state, mankind has not been shorn of its humanity.

With regard to the third question, when the New Testament refers to the new creation, it speaks of the restoration of the image (see 1 Cor. 15:49, 2 Cor. 3:18). This is the central emphasis in Pauline anthropology. Regeneration and sanctification renew the believer after the image of his or her Creator. God has predestined the redeemed to be conformed to the image of Christ (see Rom. 8:29).[12]

Of all the potential motivating drivers in life, arguably none is more powerful than to be who you were created to be, experiencing in your person the fullness of God's creation. As disciples, we are being transformed to reflect God's image more and more clearly. For those who are not yet disciples, the capacity to be creative, intelligent, aesthetic, moral, relational and spiritual, while marred by sin, still exists.

What is the responsibility of the church to young people during the formative years of life? A focus on adolescent and child capacities, under the guidance and care of mature Christian leadership, can help at-risk youth discover the source of their imagery. As they explore what it means to be created by God in His image, youth can begin to understand their significant part in the mega-story known as the kingdom of God.

Notes

1. C. F. D. Moule, *Gospel of Mark*, as cited in *The Expositor's Bible Commentary*, ed. Frank E. Gaebelein and J. D. Douglas (Grand Rapids, MI: Zondervan, 1990). Electronic text hypertexted and prepared by OakTree Software, Inc.

2. A. R. Colón with P. A. Colón, *A History of Children: A Socio-cultural Survey Across Millennia* (Westport, CT: Greenwood Press, 2001), p. 91, quoted at http://www.pobronson.com/factbook/pages/198.html#579, accessed February 2010.

3. Jawanza Kunjufu, *Countering the Conspiracy to Destroy Black Boys* (Sauk Village, IL: African American Images, 1985).

4. Maria Montessori, *The Absorbent Mind* (New York: Henry Holt and Company, 1995), p. 4.

5. Ibid., p. 7.

6. Alfred Meidow, "Maria Montessori opens the first Casa dei Bambini (Children's house)," in Daniel Schugurensky, ed., *History of Education: Selected Moments of the 20th Century*, http://schugurensky.faculty.asu.edu/moments/1907montessori.html, accessed July 2015.

7. Montessori, *The Absorbent Mind*, p. 92.

8. Scottie May, "Maria Montessori," in *Listing of Christian Educators*, Talbot School of Theology, Biola University, http://www.talbot.edu/ce20/educators/catholic/maria_montessori/, accessed July 2015.

9. Fred Smith Sr., *Leading with Integrity: Competence with Christian Character* (Bloomington, MN: Bethany House Publishers, 1999), p. 171.

10. Isaac Watts, "Alas, And Did My Savior Bleed?" originally published in *Hymns and Spiritual Songs*, 1707-09, Book II, number 9.

11. Peter May, "What Is the Image of God?" http://www.bethinking.org/human-life/what-is-the-image-of-god, accessed July 2015.

12. Charles L. Feinberg, *The Image of God*, Bibliotheca Sacra 129, Dallas Theological Seminary, 1972, pp. 235-246.

Questions for Thought

1. When you examine the youth you serve (or, for that matter, anyone else) through the grid of the divine imprint, what do you see?

2. What are some of the elements of Montessori's work that contributed to a motivational environment?

3. Clues to motivating youth can be discovered by "reading" the behaviors and responses of the youth themselves. As you examine the youth in your ministry, what clues do you find?

Chapter 9

LEADERSHIP

WHERE POTENTIAL AND HOPE IGNITE

So far we have explored three of the four concepts foundational to a transformational discipleship ministry:

1. *Mission.* Mission is more than an activity; it describes the nature and purpose of the church. Just as they were in Paul's day, cities are centers of missional activity that is carried out by God's people as they engage society. That engagement includes the world of urban youth—a segment of society that is both deeply loved by God and dangerously marginalized and vulnerable.

2. *Growing Up Urban.* At the heart of the adolescent journey is a search for identity. Urban youth take this journey under the pressure of an environment saturated by violence, crime, instability and fear. As youth are forced to adapt to the code of the street, their search for identity becomes altered and is often corrupted. Urban realities force the "Who am I and why am I here?" quest to be overridden by the more immediate: "How do I survive?" In the process, a new identity emerges—one often marked by hopelessness and (for many) a resignation to thuggery and street life.

3. *Divine Imprint.* Deep within each person lies a divine imprint—a set of qualities that uniquely reflect the nature

of God in him or her. Because all human beings are created in God's image, creation provides the key to personal
motivation. For the adolescent in search of identity, becoming the person he or she was created to be and growing into that awareness is a powerful motivator. So the
key to motivating youth is awakening and nurturing their
divine imprint. The missional task among urban adolescents is to help them discover what they are already wired
to seek: their God-endowed uniqueness and identity.

These foundational concepts inform the purpose and nature of
youth ministry:

- The tendency is to engage in youth ministry because of
  the needs of parents, churches and/or communities. Youth
  programming provides healthy activities for kids and
  keeps them out of trouble, which for parents and adults is
  a good thing. Focusing on the pillars of transformational discipleship, however, creates a different motivation:
  The primary drive for ministry becomes the felt needs of
  youth themselves.
- The concepts of mission and growing up urban make ministry among inner-city youth a kingdom of God impera-
  tive. From a strategic standpoint, youth will soon be adults
  and play significant roles in society's future. The growth
  of gang violence and civil unrest in cities all over the world
  provides a glimpse into that future. It is not a pretty sight.
  Yet, as a friend and mentor once said, "What a tremendous
  opportunity!" While the world wrestles with a socio-political response, the church has been empowered to foster
  transformative change.
- Felt need shapes ministry strategy. If adolescence as a phase
  in human development is by God's design, responding to
  the primary need of adolescents is key to effective ministry.

What is that need? Returning to the words of tennis pro
Andre Agassi: "Image. . . is everything." The need for
identity discovery should influence the purpose of youth
ministry. That purpose becomes *to create an environment in
which youth can discover who they are in Christ.*

The final concept takes the first three and moves them from
theory to practice. Youth become engaged in missional activity.
Growing up urban shifts from an inescapable oppression to an
experience to be studied, understood and conquered. The divine
imprint comes alive in the human experience.

All of this takes place in the life of the adolescent through the
fourth concept of transformational discipleship: leadership.

Leading and Learning

When I was in seminary, a fellow student once looked me in the
eye and said, "*You* are a natural leader." At first his comment struck
me as strange. But as I continued to think about it, I realized he
might be right. Throughout grade school, my field of interest was
music. I played the trombone and sang. I immersed myself in a
variety of musical activities: band, choir, orchestras, small singing
and instrumental ensembles, competitions, and the yearly school
musical. In many of these contexts, I played a leadership role. In
college there was not much time to lead, but I did direct a small
jazz ensemble (affectionately known as "Tiny" Band).

My leadership experience only increased after I became
a Christian. In my first year, I assisted in leading a high school
youth club. I co-taught and later taught the high school Sunday
School class. Two years later, I was a student at Denver Seminary.
While there I served as a church choir director and youth pastor.
I led teams in and out of Eastern Europe during a summer mis-
sions trip. I was in my fourth year at seminary when I founded
Neighborhood Ministries.

So my classmate was right: Leading seemed to come naturally to me. But my first experience as a Christian leader taught me an unexpected lesson—one that later fueled my interest in transformational discipleship. This lesson involved the relationship between *leading* and *learning*.

I was three months into my new life, still basking in the joy of being a Christian, when a college student from the chapel approached me. She and another female college student had established a program for kids attending the chapel and the local English-language school. About half of the group's members were boys, which forced the leaders to seek out male helpers. They recruited me and another guy from the chapel to join their leadership team.

Leading this group of kids created a strange and unexpected dynamic. I was 21 years old—barely four years older than the youth I was leading. And I was a new Christian—newer than most of them! Immersed in my newfound faith, I grew quickly. Soon I became keenly aware that, in terms of growth, I was but one step ahead of them.

The high school students saw this as well. From their perspective, my being the same age spiritually, yet growing at a faster pace, motivated them to take their faith seriously. This was the dynamic: Leadership of young people by a young person stimulated all of us to grow in our relationship with Christ. It was a moment of great excitement—one many of us look back on with great joy to this day.

This dynamic is recreated in the transformational discipleship experience. High school students lead the elementary program throughout the school year. During that time, the children may not view their young leaders as anything curious. But when summer comes, and those same high school students are leading the camp, the implications begin to seep in: "These leaders are only a few years older than me. . . . They are not gang leaders or drug pushers or dropouts; they are strong leaders. . . . Could this experience be in *my* future?"

A similar dynamic takes place in the high school leaders. During the school year, they take turns leading the elementary program. They may find this interesting and different and fun. But when the summer day camp starts, they begin to feel the weight of leadership. Children open up to them in ways they did not expect. Discussions at staff meetings move beyond curriculum or activity plans or discipline problems to issues of relationships and counseling and ethics. Suddenly leadership begins to matter. Character matters. The youth leaders have younger lives in their hands. They begin to take that seriously.

Potential and hope ignite when children see—modeled in youth from their neighborhood—possibilities for their own lives. This is the fruit of youth leadership.

Misconceptions

Misconceptions regarding leadership abound. We've already mentioned a few of them:

- Leaders are born and not made. True leaders, like cream, will rise to the top on their own.
- Adolescents lack the maturity to lead. Their greater need is for biblical knowledge imparted in love. Instruction and love are enough.
- Youth experience leadership development by fulfilling assigned responsibilities. Completing tasks with a positive attitude is a sign of leadership potential that can blossom later in life.

Young people have their own misconceptions about leadership. Few view themselves as leaders. They tend to place leadership mantles on those holding special positions, such as quarterback or head cheerleader or president of the chess club. Unless you have a title, you are not a leader.

Many divide the world into two groups: leaders and followers. "Where are you going, and who's following you?" "If you are going someplace and no one is following you, you're just out for a walk." These statements accentuate the "command and control" side of leadership. It is an important dimension. Inherent in leadership is the ability to command.

But this does not mean that one label defines us: leader or follower. A low-level manager leads the people within his/her division while reporting to those higher on the organizational chart. A parent may work for someone else on the job, but must still provide guidance and direction at home. An otherwise timid child might bring kids on the block together for a game of stickball.

The leader/follower dichotomy is too simplistic. It can create one-way communication and a false sense of superiority/inferiority. A more comprehensive view of leadership is needed. John Maxwell defines leadership in this way: "Leadership is influence: nothing more, nothing less." Bobb Biehl defines leadership as knowing what to do next, knowing why that is important, and knowing how to bring appropriate resources to bear on the need at hand. Everyone—to some degree, at different times, within various dimensions of life—leads.

Most church leaders believe in transformation. Yet few press this important value into the internal workings of their ministries. In 1 Corinthians 12, Paul talks about spiritual gifts. Discovering and utilizing one's gifts is transforming, both to the individual and in the contribution made to the vitality of the Christian community. Yet more often than not, neither transformation nor the interplay of gifts finds its way into the life of leadership teams.

In his book *My Way or the Highway: The Micromanagement Survival Guide*, performance improvement specialist Harry Chambers describes the core ethic of the micromanager, which I would summarize with these three phrases:

I'm the boss.
I own you.
You owe me.

Sadly, this philosophy of leadership is far too prevalent among Christian organizations today. It is a major barrier to transformational discipleship.

Youth Leaders

There is a difference between transactional and transformational leadership. Transactional leadership is product- and reward-oriented. The subordinate is rewarded for following directives and producing a desired product. In this sense, being a leader means to "do": to make decisions and instruct others.

But leadership is more than transactions. Leadership is visionary. It inspires. It triggers internal motivations and rallies people around a common cause. John F. Kennedy engendered this kind of leadership when he said, "Some look at things as they are and ask, 'Why?' I dream of things that could be and ask, 'Why not?'" The transformational leader lifts his/her sights beyond self-interest to the needs of others. In this sense, leadership means to "be": to focus on the development of others, helping individuals maximize their leadership potential.

The dimension most critical to effective leadership development among youth is transformation. Education specialists Josephine van Linden and Carl Fertman highlight this point in their book *Youth Leadership: A Guide to Understanding Leadership Development in Adolescents*. They characterize leadership in this way:

> For our purpose, we define leaders as individuals (both adults and adolescents) who think for themselves, communicate their thoughts and feelings to others, and help others understand and act on their own beliefs; they

influence others in an ethical and socially responsible way. For many, leadership is best described as a physical sensation: a need to share ideas, energy, and creativity, and not let personal insecurities be an obstacle. Being a leader means trusting one's instincts, both when doing leadership tasks and being a leader.[1]

Note the action phrases: "think for themselves," "communicate their thoughts and feelings," "help others understand and act," "influence others," "share ideas, energy, and creativity," and "trusting one's instincts." Transformational leaders reach beyond the completion of tasks to the enriching of lives.

This places several important priorities on the youth leadership experience:

- *Tasks must be significant.* Montessori discovered this in her work with children. "The essential thing is for the task to arouse such an interest that it engages the child's whole personality."[2] Remember the illustration of the construction foreman who asked workers what they were doing? All three deemed their work as important, but only one ("I'm building a cathedral") was driven by a vision that went beyond necessity to significance: the difference made over a lifetime. For tasks to be transformational, they must be significant to the ones performing them.
- *Vision must be shared.* Transactional leadership focuses on the task that is of importance to the leader. Transformational leadership focuses on tasks tied to a vision that is shared by everyone involved. Leaders and those they are leading are on a shared adventure. Tasks are significant as part of a bigger plan and greater purpose.
- *Divine imprints must be explored.* Tasks become transformational when they provide glimpses into youths'

individual strengths, inclinations and capacities. The task is important partly because in pursuing it, young leaders discover important truths about themselves.

Leadership in the Bible

Leaders and leadership fill the pages of Scripture. There are leaders of tribes, families and nations. Many are chosen or appointed. Apart from Abijah's reference to God as a leader (see 2 Chronicles 13:12), the term "leader" is used to describe people. New Testament writers refer to the head of the synagogue as "the synagogue leader" (Matthew 9:18; Luke 13:14; Acts 18:8,17).

Every style of leadership is found in the Scriptures. There are those who favored an autocratic style (for example, Saul and Nebuchadnezzar) and those who were more participative (such as Moses, at the advice of his father-in-law, Jethro). Many leaders mentioned in the book of Judges were *laissez-faire*, in contrast to Nehemiah and Peter, who both exercised strong functional and transactional leadership qualities. Arguably, examples of transformational leadership would be King David and the apostle Paul.

There are passages that speak to leadership character (see Jeremiah 3:15; 1 Peter 5:3; Philippians 2:3; 2 Corinthians 10:12-18; Romans 12:3), as well as those that describe leadership tasks (see 2 Timothy 4:5; Galatians 6:1; Romans 13:7; Titus 2:15) and motivations (see 1 Peter 5:2; Romans 12:8). There are also passages encouraging proper attitudes towards church leaders (see Hebrews 13:17; 1 Timothy 5:17; 1 Thessalonians 5:12-13).

A focus on the positive leaders (though there are certainly plenty of negative ones) in the Scriptures reveals a number of common characteristics:

- The focus of their leadership is a God-given task upon which they bring their skills and leadership traits to bear.
- There is a burden or need that must be met.

- Their burden drives them to utilize existing skills, develop necessary ones, and/or recruit others who possess the skills needed.
- They act out of God-shaped character; it is the combination of godly character, commitment, knowledge and skills that commands authority and respect from others.
- They approach tasks with a sense of responsibility—almost destiny. They *know* that this (whatever it is) is something they must do.

What seems less significant is the scope or magnitude of the leadership task. Some led vast numbers of people, while others counseled individual family members (as Mordecai did with Esther) or acted on behalf of sick friends (see Luke 5:18-19). Another relatively insignificant issue is age. While elders in Scripture seemed to be the oldest and wisest men of the village, there are many examples of the mantle of leadership falling on younger individuals—such as Joshua, David, Esther, Jeremiah, Josiah and Timothy.

One cannot embrace discipleship without leading in some way, shape or form. And, as Paul's letters to Timothy reveal, it is while engaged in the process of leading (Timothy was "on the job" when he received Paul's instruction) that learning and growth take place. Paul's epistles may be instructional in nature, yet his approach to discipleship and leadership development went beyond instruction to dialogue, shared experiences and role modeling.

Leadership Dimensions

There are three dimensions of leadership that are crucial to the transformational discipleship process:

1. Servant Leadership

> Jesus called them together and said, "You know that those
> who are regarded as rulers of the Gentiles lord it over them,
> and their high officials exercise authority over them. Not so
> with you. Instead, whoever wants to become great among
> you must be your servant, and whoever wants to be first
> must be slave of all. For even the Son of Man did not come
> to be served, but to serve, and to give his life as a ransom
> for many" (Mark 10:42-45).

Jesus reminded His disciples what the conventions of leadership were in their day. It essentially amounted to tyranny. Greatness was defined as power—coercive power. Jesus categorically
rejected this style of leadership. He made three statements that
grew in intensity: (1) to be great one must serve; (2) to be first one
must be slave to all; and (3) this leadership philosophy is exempli-
fied in me. In the kingdom of God, greatness is not achieved by the
assertion of rank but through humble service.

"*Whoever wants to become great among you must be your servant,
and whoever wants to be first must be slave of all.*" To be great, one must
serve; to be first, one must be slave to all. How is that possible in
today's world? How can the CEO or president of a modern-day
organization function as a servant leader—one who serves and is
"slave" to all?

I believe the answer lies in the nature of *authority*. Jesus said
the high priests "exercised authority" over others. This expression
comes from a single Greek term that means "to domineer." Matthew uses a different word to describe Jesus' leadership:

> When Jesus had finished saying these things, the crowds
> were amazed at his teaching, because he taught as one who
> had *authority*, and not as their teachers of the law (Matthew
> 7:28-29, emphasis added).

The term Matthew uses refers to power, ability or faculty. Within "authority" is the word "author," or creator. To speak with authority is to speak either as the author or by knowledgably presenting the ideas of the author. And it means doing so clearly, with integrity.

I recently had a kidney transplant. The surgery was done robotically—which sounds scary, but they say it is the safest way to perform transplants. The surgical team had performed this procedure more than 900 times! I do not know if the chief surgeon authored the method, but his extensive knowledge and experience made him an authority on the procedure.

One reason I am committed to expository preaching is that true exposition forces the preacher to find the central idea of a given passage and apply it to life. Someone once said, If you know what the biblical writer is saying and what the biblical listener is hearing, you can know what God is saying. When we rightly represent the ideas of the biblical author, our teaching and preaching come across with authority.

Far too many leaders confuse authority with power. Power can come with authority, but servant leaders do not lead with power. They lead with authority, and they do so in order to serve others.

2. Credible Leadership

Command and teach these things. Don't let anyone look down on you because you are young, but set an example for the believers in speech, in conduct, in love, in faith and in purity. Until I come, devote yourself to the public reading of Scripture, to preaching and to teaching. Do not neglect your gift, which was given you through prophecy when the body of elders laid their hands on you.

Be diligent in these matters; give yourself wholly to them, so that everyone may see your progress. Watch your life and doctrine closely. Persevere in them, because if you do, you will save both yourself and your hearers (1 Timothy 4:11-16).

Paul is writing to Timothy, his "true son in the faith" (1 Timothy 1:2). Timothy is instructed and encouraged to command and teach the church regarding conduct in keeping with faith in Christ. Effectiveness in leadership required dual attentiveness to personal piety and to the quality, behaviors and operations of church leadership (see 1 Timothy 1:18-20; 4:11).

In the passage quoted above, Paul focuses on exhorting Timothy toward godliness. Here the commands require more personal than group application. Of note is how Timothy is instructed to respond to his detractors, for whom his age was an issue. His response was to be demonstrative in nature: leading an exemplary Christian life. In essence, his authority—in keeping with young leaders throughout biblical history—was contingent upon his character, not his age.

3. Heroic Leadership

Very truly I tell you, whoever believes in me will do the works I have been doing, and they will do even greater things than these, because I am going to the Father (John 14:12).

Leadership as heroic—this is how Chris Lowney describes the Jesuit view of leadership in his book *Heroic Leadership: Best Practices from a 450-Year-Old Company that Changed the World*.

Ignatius of Loyola established an order within the Catholic Church that pressed a unique set of leadership values into a strategy that transformed cultures around the world. Those values are the following:

a. We are all leaders, and we lead all the time.
Every person has (often untapped) leadership potential. The Jesuit model rejects the "one great man" model of leadership for a simple reason: *Everyone has influence, and everyone projects influence*—good or bad, large or small—all the time.

The tendency among leadership gurus is to highlight those whose leadership intersected with great moments in history—like Winston Churchill and World War II, or Mandela during apartheid in South Africa. Leaders may rise during such times, but they do not wait for world-changing, defining-moment opportunities to come to them. Leaders seize all available opportunities to influence and make an impact. *Leadership is defined not by the scale of the opportunity but by the quality of one's response.*

b. Leadership comes from within.

A leader's most compelling asset is who he or she is: a person anchored by core beliefs, values and purpose, and who therefore faces the world with clarity and vision. This vision is more than clever words fashioned into a mission statement. It is intensely personal—the hard-won product of self-reflection: *Who am I? What do I care about? What do I want? How do I fit into the world?*

c. Leadership is not an act. It is a life.

Conventional wisdom ties leadership to tasks—thinking of it as something to be turned on or off depending on the context. But leadership is not a task or a job. *Leadership is real life.* The early Jesuits talked about *nuestro modo de proceder*: "our way of proceeding." Their actions flowed from a worldview and priorities shared by all members of the Jesuit team. Leadership was their compass for living.

d. Leadership development is an ongoing process of self-development.

The "steps to becoming a leader" messages so prevalent today are misleading. Steps may enlighten, but they do not produce a leader. Strong leaders are avid learners.

Leadership development is a never-ending work-in-progress, in need of continual maturing and growth.

These leadership principles led Jesuits to foster certain competencies:

- *Self-awareness*. They were challenged "to order one's life." Jesuits equipped recruits to succeed by molding them into leaders who understood personal strengths, weaknesses, values and worldview.
- *Ingenuity*. Jesuits equipped recruits to succeed by molding them into leaders who confidently innovated and adapted to embrace a changing world. Loyola described the ideal Jesuit as "living with one foot raised"—always ready to respond to emerging opportunities.
- *Love*. Jesuits equipped recruits to succeed by molding them into leaders who engaged others with a positive, loving attitude. Loving leaders face the world with a confident, healthy sense of themselves as endowed with talent, dignity and value. They passionately commit to honoring and unlocking potential found in themselves and others. Loving leaders create loving environments, bound and energized by loyalty, affection and mutual support.
- *Heroism*. Jesuits equipped recruits to succeed by molding them into leaders who energized themselves and others from heroic ambitions. Loyola encouraged Jesuits to "endeavor to conceive great resolves and elicit equally great desires." As with athletes, musicians or managers who focus unrelentingly on ambitious goals, heroic leaders imagine an inspiring future and

strive to shape it rather than passively watching
the future happen around them. Jesuits "elicit
great desires" by envisioning heroic objectives.[3]

What could be more heroic than to see leadership potential
come alive in the urban adolescent? If adolescents became an influence for good in children's lives, would that not be a legacy worth
leaving? That would truly be heroic!

Making a Difference

Servanthood. Credibility. Heroism. These are qualities cultivated
within the transformational discipleship ministry model. They are
fostered both within adults who lead the ministry and in adolescents
who lead the children. Over time, they shape the character and fruit-
fulness of the emerging leader. Consider these reflections from a few
alums of our transformational discipleship ministry:

- *Taking kids outside their element [on service trips to Honduras],
  showing them that there is something bigger outside their neighborhood
  that's beyond them . . . I think the experience of taking kids from what's
  considered a poor neighborhood to a more impoverished neighborhood
  is huge. That really helps kids/teenagers/young people see that they
  don't have to be viewed as victims, that I as a young person can learn
  something from someone else out there who has even less than I. And I
  can help and I can be a leader in this situation.* (Raquel)
- *What was being on staff like? Revealing. I was shy; I didn't talk much
  because I stuttered. Coming through school, kids made fun of me
  when I stuttered. I discovered I can talk. . . . I learned I was good with
  people—that I was kind of a friendly guy, big into relationships. One
  of the greatest things I learned was that I had a heart for kids who were
  growing up like me. I learned that I was able to connect.* (Jimmy)
- *I was walking with a friend after school and she was cussing.
  I looked up and saw one of my club kids. I told my friend, "You need
  to stop. This kid coming towards us is in my club program. Hanging*

out with you while you're cussing hurts my leadership. Stop or I'll
have to leave." (Skye)

- *I think that experience [Honduras] was huge, huge for them (and me) . . . being on those trips with the kids and seeing them grow . . . being put in very uncomfortable situations, and just seeing them struggle with it. "How am I going to get through this experience: to calm myself down because my luggage is lost, or I've never been on a plane before, or I'm in a third-world country and there are people walking around with machine guns. . . how do I deal with that?" To see that life is bigger than them, and see God working outside their neighborhood? Huge.* (Raquel)

I am reminded again of Skye's description of the difference between the leadership programs at her high school and the leadership experience at Neighborhood Ministries: "There they *talk* about leadership. Here you *do* it."

It is through leading that clarity of purpose and identity come to life. Leadership takes discipleship values and embeds them into the life and psyche of the leader. Leadership turns ideas into real-life experiences. Head knowledge becomes street knowledge; verbal assent gives way to transformative action.

Leadership pulls mission, growing up urban, and the divine imprint together into a powerful adventure of growth, discovery and influence within the adolescent experience. Armed with the knowledge of who they are in Christ, young leaders can move confidently beyond high school into the God-shaped future awaiting them.

Notes

1. Josephine A. van Linden and Carl I. Fertman, *Youth Leadership: A Guide to Understanding Leadership in Adolescents* (San Francisco: Jossey-Bass Publishers, 1998), p. 17.
2. Maria Montessori, as quoted in History of Education: Selected Moments of the 20th Century, Daniel Schugurensky, ed., http://schugurensky.faculty.asu.edu/moments/1907montessori.html, accessed November 2009.
3. Chris Lowney, *Heroic Leadership: Best Practices from a 450-year-old Company that Changed the World* (Chicago, IL: Loyola Press, 2003).

Questions for Thought

1. What assumptions do you have about leadership that hinder your ability or desire to pursue a youth leadership component in your ministry?

2. How would you describe your leadership style? Autocratic? Participative? Laissez-faire? Transactional? Transformational?

3. Do you lead with power or authority? What changes need to be made in order for you to lead with authority?

4. Are you a credible leader? How does your example match up to Paul's list in 1 Timothy 4:12?

5. Is your leadership heroic? Does it "elicit great desires"? What is heroic about your ministry?

6. "There they talk about leadership. Here you do it." Can any of your youth say this? Would you like them to?

Chapter 10

TIME TO RUN

*Write down the revelation and make it plain on tablets
so that a herald may run with it.*

HABAKKUK 2:2

Habakkuk is unique among the Old Testament prophets. He is a prophet, to be sure. His heart aches over the lawlessness and wickedness of Israel. He expects God to judge the nation. He pleads with God to make things right.

Yet his prophecy does not include the "Thus saith the Lord!" clarion call one expects from a prophet. It reads more like a personal journal—a private conversation with God. God's decision to use the inexorable Babylonian invasion to discipline the nation had shaken Habakkuk. It seemed inconsistent—frighteningly out of character—with God's nature. The result was a momentary crisis of faith. Habakkuk cried out to God:

> Your eyes are too pure to look on evil;
>   you cannot tolerate wrongdoing.
> Why then do you tolerate the treacherous?
>   Why are you silent while the wicked
>   swallow up those more righteous than themselves?
>   (Habakkuk 1:13).

One cannot engage urban youth for any meaningful length of time without experiencing momentary crises of faith. The realities of the urban experience—with its chronic web of brokenness, violence and disappointment—can at times overwhelm even the most valiant of Christian leaders. I have heard the righteous cry out in bewilderment: "God, where are You? Why do You tolerate [fill in the blank]?"

God responds:

Write down the revelation and make it plain on tablets . . .

Habakkuk was given a revelation—a vision that extended beyond Israel's impending captivity to the restoration of the Jews' freedom and the demise of their oppressors. Strangely, it began with a command: *Write it down.* Why?

Most communicators appreciate the clarity that comes from writing. Educators within every known discipline acknowledge this: Thoughts that cannot be clearly expressed on a page remain stubbornly obscure. Seventeenth-century English statesman and philosopher Francis Bacon observed:

Reading maketh a full man;
Speaking a ready man;
Writing an exact man.

So it is understandable that God would tell Habakkuk to write the revelation down. The promise preserved in writing would encourage the soon-to-be captive. It would help sustain the oppressed throughout a time of suffering.

The next statement, though, is peculiar: ". . . *so that a herald [the one who reads] may run with it.*" Why "run"? What does this mean?

The Hebrew language is filled with nuances—shades of meaning. One scholar suggests that the writing was to be so clear that a person on the run could read the message. Another commentator views the word "run" as a poetic device pointing to one's ability to live (walk, run) according to the will of God. Still another proposes that "runners" were all who passed by and read the message aloud to the illiterate.[1]

Most striking to me is God's expectation that they "run" in the first place! Somehow the clearly written message would enable the people of God to successfully "run" during their captivity. The message was clear, the promise absolute. While they could not stop the Babylonian invasion, God's revelation would empower them to persevere.

In chapter three, Habakkuk offers a prayer. He begins by remembering who God is ("I have heard of your fame"). He worships Him ("I stand in awe of your deeds"). He expects God to act ("Repeat them in our day"). He trusts God to love even through hard times ("In wrath remember mercy").

He ends his prayer with a profoundly hopeful statement:

> Though the fig tree does not bud
>   and there are no grapes on the vines,
> though the olive crop fails
>   and the fields produce no food,
> though there are no sheep in the pen
>   and no cattle in the stalls,
> yet I will rejoice in the LORD,
>   I will be joyful in God my Savior (Habakkuk 3:17-18).

No amount of suffering would vanquish his joy. His response was simple: *faithfulness*. He would be faithful to God. And notice what that faithfulness would look like:

> The Sovereign LORD is my strength;
>   he makes my feet like the feet of a deer,
>   he enables me to tread on the heights (Habakkuk 3:19).

With "the feet of a deer" he would "tread on the heights." Trusting God, he would run.

Running with Reshaping Urban Discipleship

Shelly and I enjoy Saturday mornings—our weekly time for shared devotions and prayer. Currently we are reading excerpts from Rueben Job's *When You Pray: Daily Practices for Prayerful Living*. Last week's reading reminded me how important the reshaping of urban youth discipleship is:

> Want to follow Jesus? Go where the wounds are, for that is where Jesus went. Demon possessed, paralyzed, blind, cut off from family and community, ostracized and left out, ridiculed and harassed, divided and estranged, these were the ones who seem to draw the very presence of Jesus. . . .
>
> We don't have to be particularly observant to notice that our world is filled with the wounded and broken. While many of them may feel forgotten, estranged, ridiculed, and left out, they are the very ones to whom Jesus comes to bring healing, hope, and wholeness.
>
> Would you like to experience a new level of effectiveness and faithfulness? Go where the wounds are. This is what Jesus did and that is what Jesus does today. Let's meet him there today and every day and be a part of his life-giving ministry.[2]

To enter urban ministry is to go where the wounds are. Urban youth grow up in a culture of violence. Christians working off old assumptions—perhaps the most careless being the idea that "the cream will rise" (i.e., that those youth "destined" to survive the harsh life of the streets will somehow survive)—in effect limit children's access to Jesus. The disconnect between our assumptions and the growing youth unrest in cities all over the world is staggering. Most Christian leaders would rather address problems after they've taken root (in the adult) than at their point of origin (in children and adolescents).

Access to Jesus may be limited, yet youth seem to have full access to the destructive forces of urban dysfunction, hopelessness and death. The church is called to be salt and light in the midst of such circumstances. Transformational discipleship creates an oasis in the urban desert—a safe space in which generations of youth can engage Jesus and discover who they are in Christ.

So far we have spent our time rethinking how the church engages urban youth:

- We have defined transformational discipleship as *an approach to youth ministry centered on maximizing the adolescent leadership experience in ways that mold youth for future service and motivate the future leaders (children) these adolescents influence.*
- The mission of a transformational discipleship ministry is *to create an environment in which youth can discover who they are in Christ.*
- The vision of a transformational discipleship ministry is *to see transformation in the heart of the city, where youth grow in faith and confidence to serve others, starting with the children of their neighborhood, reaching as far as God's purpose for their lives takes them.*
- What drives transformational discipleship is a foundational set of socio-theological concepts: (1) *mission as the identity and purpose of the church,* (2) *urban youth as a focus of neighbor-love and discipleship,* (3) *the image of God as key to personal motivation and societal contribution,* and (4) *leadership as the activity in which discipleship, identity discovery and life purpose come alive in the adolescent experience.*

I believe that the application of these ideas will empower youth ministries to run. As we allow our understanding of urban discipleship to be reshaped, leaders will experience a renewed sense of hope, purpose and power. We will set in motion formative change that will have an impact on multiple generations of youth. Then the reality we long for will come alive in the urban experience: transformation in the heart of the city.

God does not want us to be bewildered or stagnant in serving the urban youth population. I believe that the concepts foundational to transformational discipleship will give leaders "the feet of a deer" so that we might "tread on the heights." My prayer is that as we trust God's perspective on mission, urban youth, the divine imprint and leadership, He will empower urban leaders to make a qualitative difference in the lives of urban youth.

The time has come for us to *run*.

Notes

1. Ralph L. Smith, *Word Biblical Commentary: Micah - Malachi Vol. 32* (Nashville, TN: Thomas Nelson, 1984), p. 105.
2. Rueben P. Job, *When You Pray: Daily Practices for Prayerful Living* (Nashville, TN: Abingdon Press, 2009), p. 130.

Praxis

From Theory to Substance

He who does that which he sees, shall understand; he who is set upon understanding rather than doing, shall go on stumbling and mistaking and speaking foolishness.

GEORGE MacDONALD

How do we do it? How do we move from theology to practice, from thought to accomplishment? How do we press the transformational discipleship philosophy into the fabric of ministry?

To meet the challenges of a changing world, we must be prepared to change everything about ourselves except our fundamental core beliefs. This requires an ability to distinguish between belief and practice. *We must commit to reaffirming core values through a continual refining and improving upon the ways in which we live out our central beliefs.*

With this in mind, this section will do three things:

1. *Present an overarching framework of the developmental process.* This framework is based upon starting a transformational discipleship ministry from scratch. It only addresses those elements related to transformational discipleship, not any specialized ministry emphasis, such as education, music, sports, the arts, etc. This framework can be applied to all types of youth ministries.

2. *Identify the values being fleshed out within each phase of the developmental process.* Knowing the why of each phase presses meaning and purpose into what will be an extended process. Your values, if they are genuine, will motivate and sustain you over the long haul.

3. *Share practices vital to each phase of the developmental process.* These practices grew out of my personal experiences in animating leadership capacity and leading a youth

development ministry. While important, they are neither sacrosanct nor exhaustive. It is my hope that those who are reading and applying this philosophy will build upon the things I have learned and discover new ways to transform the lives of urban youth.

Phases at a Glance

Transformational discipleship is a long-term process. It engages young people as they move through three distinct phases of pre-adult life.

- *Late Childhood.* Most people understand childhood as that period of life between toddlerhood and early adolescence—ages 5 through 11. There are reasons the youth developer should begin with the *later childhood* phase—ages 8 through 11, or third through fifth grade. These reasons have to do with Jawanza Kunjufu's description of the Fourth Grade Failure Syndrome. It is around the fourth grade that the realities of "minority status" in relation to the larger world begin to affect the black child's psyche. Bobb Biehl, in his insightful work *4th Grade,* also pinpoints this age as a significant life-shaping moment for all children. Early childhood is important, but a focus on third through fifth grade reaches children at a critical time of life, adding motivation to young emerging leaders to be an influence for good among this significant age group.
- *Early Adolescence.* Early adolescence—ages 12 through 14— is where young people exhibit the first waves of "Sturm und Drang" (storm and stress), the internal confusion and erratic behavior associated with the adolescent's journey toward adulthood. It is during this phase that the transformational discipleship developer forges a culture of discipleship by embedding the practice of thinking,

questioning, and intentionally engaging life issues—always exploring the question "Where is God in all this?"—within the youth program.

- *Adolescence.* Once early adolescents reach high school—entering the *adolescence* phase of life—they are invited to join the Emerging Leaders. They have grown accustomed to thinking, asking questions, and looking for God in the context of life. Now, as adolescents, they embrace the added responsibility of teaching and leading children in the later childhood stage. For the emerging leaders, the group or "club" experience takes on the qualities of a team—or a task force. They are challenged, throughout their high school group experience, to commit (1) *to grow in their knowledge of who they are in Christ,* (2) *to lead the weekly elementary program and summer day camp,* and (3) *to submit as much as they know about themselves to as much as they know about Jesus Christ.*

There are three developmental phases to building a transformational discipleship ministry:

Developmental Phases of Transformational Discipleship

Phase 1: Context	Phase 2: Culture	Phase 3: Leadership
Identity Neighbor Kingdom	Decode Model Harambee	The Emerging Leaders Initiative

- The *Context* phase focuses on the *positioning* of the ministry in relation to youth, the local community and the Christian church.

- The *Culture* phase focuses on *practices* that shape the environment in which youth can discover who they are in Christ.
- The *Leadership* phase focuses on the *capacity discovery* and *leadership development* of adolescents who participate in the Emerging Leaders Initiative.

The phases are interconnected. One cannot establish the right culture outside the proper context. It is the transforming discipleship culture that cultivates the thought processes, hopes and motivations needed for adolescents to succeed as emerging leaders.

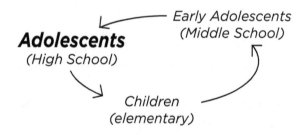

A cycle develops. Adolescent leaders influence children, who move through middle school with the hope of one day becoming like the adolescents who influenced them. *"Potential and hope ignite when children see—modeled in youth from their neighborhood—possibilities for their own lives."*

Chapter 11

C O N T E X T

IDENTITY, NEIGHBOR, KINGDOM

How you position yourself within the context of your ministry will have an impact on the effectiveness of your ministry. For this reason, the first phase of a transformational discipleship ministry is context. Context is about right beginnings in the areas of identity, positioning and role. It is about your relationship to youth, your neighbors and the Church. It is about answering the question "Who are you in relation to what you do and the people you seek to influence?" All of this requires intentionality, because if you are not intentional about defining yourself, others will do it for you.

Defining Purpose

Purpose is important to understanding identity. Leaders owe it to themselves and their constituents (youth, co-leaders, supporters, etc.) to establish a clear sense of purpose.

A well-defined understanding of purpose:

- fosters team unity in pursuit of shared goals
- helps clarify assumptions
- enables interested outsiders to respond with a strong "Yes, this is something I want to be part of!" or a strong "No, this is not for me."
- reveals uniqueness, i.e., the specific role your mission plays in God's larger kingdom agenda

Your ministry's definition of purpose is best expressed in a *mission statement*. A mission statement includes three key elements: (1) your name, (2) your classification or identity label, and (3) your purpose (the reason you exist).

For example:

- "Freedom Sports (name) is a community sports program (identity label) that exists to build Christian character in urban youth through sports (purpose statement)."
- "Neighborhood Ministries (name) is a Christian youth development agency (identity) that exists to unleash the leadership potential of youth residing in northeast Denver (purpose)."

Mission statements should reflect true convictions—and a good one will be the outcome of careful and strenuous thought. Crafting a mission statement is hard work, but well worth the effort.

Once you define purpose, your purpose will define you.

In other words, once you have a strong mission statement in place, you will begin to ask questions such as "How does this activity fit with our purpose?" and "Will pursuing this idea advance the mission?" Any program addition or change being considered—activities, ideas, projects and even partnerships—will fall under the scrutiny of your mission statement. Knowing who you are guides you toward discovering what you must do.

Defining Program

Defining program should be more than listing a series of activities or events. For an informed understanding of program, definitions should include an explanation of both content and process.

Content lists the activities that make up your program. *Process*, however, gives meaning to those activities by explaining their sequence and outcome. Process will explain *how* activities fit together, the *logic* behind the progression, and, most important, the anticipated *result(s)*.

For example, a weekly youth meeting might consist of four components (taken from a Youth for Christ model):

- Ice-breaker (a game or fun activity)
- Discovery (an activity designed to introduce the session's topic)
- Discussion
- Talk-to (share biblical perspective)

Defining process involves explaining the purpose and desired outcome of each component:

Ice-Breaker	Discovery	Discussion	Talk-to
Purpose: group fun	**Purpose:** introduce topic	**Purpose:** honest discussion; surface youth perspective	**Purpose:** summarize discussion; present God's perspective (single idea)
Result: group cohesion	**Result:** stir thinking	**Result:** engagement; honest Q&A	**Result:** rethinking perspective in light of God's Word

Each component of the meeting has a purpose and a desired result. Defining process ties separate activities together into a logical sequence that leads to a primary result—in this case the *rethinking of perspective*. This fits with the focus of a transformational youth meeting: communicating the gospel in terms youth understand, and dealing with misconceptions of the Christian faith.

Defining Organization

I keep an arrow with me. Not a literal one, but a diagram shaped like an arrow. Written on it in small print are telling statements about our ministry. These statements fall into the following categories:

- Burden: problems we care deeply about; deficiencies in the sphere of reaching urban youth that evoke anger and make us weep
- Purpose: why we exist
- Objectives: areas of involvement necessary to fulfilling our purpose
- Milestones: accomplishments and achievements
- Ideas: possibilities for the future
- Roadblocks: top barriers to reaching our goals
- Resources: greatest resources available to help achieve our goals
- Goals: specific and doable targets acting as stair steps to fulfilling our mission

For years, I posted this huge "Masterplanning Arrow" on my office wall. Visitors who lingered in front of it caught a snapshot of Neighborhood's organizational strategy: who we are, why we exist, where we have been, where we are going, and how we plan to get there.

This was the gift Masterplanning Group International gave to me: the basic tools I needed to think and act strategically and presidentially about developing a Christian organization. With their permission, I have shared this gift with hundreds of urban leaders whose leadership capacities were enhanced as a result.

Masterplanning is a tool I use to run my ministry. It continues to serve me well. There may be strategic planning tools more suitable for you. It is important to find one that will maximize your leadership capacity.

Defining Values

Values drive actions. They answer the question "Why?"—a defining element of identity. They are our assumptions—the things we believe to be true—about the ministry.

T. J. Watson Jr., former chairman of the board of IBM, offered these thoughts about the importance of organizational values:

> It is IBM's credo that any organization, in order to survive and to achieve success, must have a sound set of beliefs on which it bases all its policies and actions.
>
> But more important than having a set of beliefs is faithful adherence to those beliefs. If any organization is to meet the challenges of a changing world, it must be prepared to change everything about itself, except those beliefs, as it moves through its present to its future.
>
> Let me reiterate. The basic philosophy, the very spirit and drive of an organization, has far more to do with its relative achievements than do technical or economic resources, organizational structure, innovation, and timing.[1]

In the early years of its existence, Neighborhood Ministries created two statements that conveyed our unique set of values. We call these our "Core Values" and "Unifying Principles."

Core Values

1. God defines worldview.

"In the beginning God created the heavens and the earth" (Genesis 1:1).

Created in the image of the living God, all people possess intrinsic value, purpose and meaning. One's purpose is fully realized only through a salvific encounter and ongoing relationship with God through His Son, Jesus Christ. In such relationship, God leads and empowers people to be all they were meant to be.

2. Motivation for ministry flows out of commitment to the Great Command.

"The most important one," answered Jesus, "is this: 'Hear, O Israel: the Lord our God, the Lord is one. Love the Lord your God with all your heart and with all your soul and with all your mind and with all your strength.' The second is this: 'Love your neighbor as yourself.' There is no commandment greater than these" (Mark 12:29-31).

The overflowing love of God that brought about creation is the same love that motivates and shapes ministry. We come into relationship with people, particularly the poor, as an overflow of the love of God toward them and us. We love others as God has loved us, and within that context invite others to become as we are: friends and servants of the living God.

3. The primary people-group we exist to serve is the at-risk youth population of northeast Denver.

"Whoever heard me spoke well of me, and those who saw me commended me, because I rescued the poor who cried for help, and the fatherless who had none to assist them" (Job 29:11-12).

It is around the felt needs of this segment of northeast Denver's residential poor that Neighborhood Ministries shapes its programs and strategies.

This core value keeps Neighborhood anchored to an indispensable mark of Christian character and credibility. In the face of gentrification, Neighborhood models this dimension of Christ-centered living to its new neighbors. Neighborhood follows the strategy of Jesus, who, as I have often heard John Perkins say, "ministered to the rich on His way to the poor."

This value also impacts the makeup of Neighborhood's leadership team. Leadership birthed from the at-risk population, especially those raised up through Neighborhood Ministries, will intentionally play prominent roles in the leadership of the ministry.

4. Strategies and methodologies are shaped by the Incarnation.

"The Word became flesh and made his dwelling among us" (John 1:14).

"Put into practice what you learned from me, what you heard and saw and realized. Do that, and God, who makes everything work together, will work you into his most excellent harmonies" (Philippians 4:9, THE MESSAGE*).*

The Incarnation is both miracle and model: God's method of salvation models how we are to reach others. Jesus—the Word—became flesh and dwelt among us. The apostle Paul adopted this model as he spent extended time in communities (see Acts 19:8-10; 20:31)—and invited people to imitate him as he did Christ (see 1 Corinthians 11:1).

This model demands character worthy of imitation. The pursuit of Christian maturity must be a priority for those serving with Neighborhood Ministries. Staff must strive to dwell in the community and among people in ways that allow for the examination and imitation of their lives. This also means, ideally, making the community home—the place where staff raise their families and love their neighbors.

Unifying Principles

1. Motivation: The Glory of God

Our motivation for ministry shall flow first and foremost out of a desire to see God glorified. As ambassadors for Christ, our love and commitment to the poor shall reflect the concern and love of God our Father. We care because He cares, and our desire shall be that His love manifest itself through us before a watching world.

2. Relationships: Affirming Mutual Dignity

We shall affirm—in thought, speech and behavior—the reality that man was created by God in the image of God. Bearing God's image, all people—children, adults, neighbors, friends, even enemies—are to be highly regarded and treated with dignity. As co-workers, we shall affirm one another in love, and love our neighbor as ourselves. In the realm of human relations, our actions shall be governed, not by partiality or prejudice, but by that divine mercy and love which alone breaks down racial, social, economic, national and other barriers.

3. Finances: Stewardship with Integrity

As stewards of God's resources, we shall handle all money matters with integrity. We shall perform our ministry duties in a manner worthy of people's financial support. We shall diligently maintain biblical and ethical standards in all matters pertaining to support raising, financial administration and fiscal accountability.

4. Work: A Faithful Pursuit of Excellence

Because God has made us co-laborers with Him, and has called and empowered us to serve the poor, we shall continually measure our ministry performance—both personal and corporate—against the standard of faithfulness and excellence. We shall faithfully carry out all duties related to our mission, and strive for excellence in everything we do.

5. Purpose: To Restore a Community

The "walls" of our neighborhood—those structures that provide health and safety and positive growth for a community—have been torn down (see Nehemiah 1:3). Our vision is to see our community restored, and to witness community residents, empowered by God, making a lasting difference in the quality of life in their neighborhood. All ministry efforts shall contribute to this greater purpose, to the glory of God.

In 2010, when Jimmy returned to Denver to continue the ministry he had started in Dallas, Neighborhood Ministries handed its youth and staff over to him. So Neighborhood Ministries as a local youth program is no more. But throughout the time we were a local agency, these statements were posted in our reception area. As with the Masterplanning Arrow, they served as lenses through which visitors could better understand our ministry. They answered the underlying question, "Why?"

The Context of Neighbor

We have devoted significant attention to neighboring and the importance of positioning yourself as a neighbor in the community you serve.

But let's step back for a moment to ask, What makes a person a neighbor? Locale? Accessibility? Proximity? What do neighbors have in common? Do children attend the same schools? Do people shop at the same stores, or hang out at local coffee shops and restaurants? Are neighbors equally impacted by the dangers associated with drug and gang activity? Do they face the same forms of institutional neglect and infrastructure deterioration? Neighbors share these things and more.

The position from which to exert the maximum influence in the lives of young people is as a neighbor—a fellow member of the community. To establish yourself as a neighbor:

- *Move.* If you have not already done so, make the neighborhood your home.
- *Get to know your neighbors.* Be accessible enough for them to know you.
- *Hang out.* Frequent local coffee shops, basketball courts, community centers and other youth hot-spots.
- *Listen.* Ask questions and pay attention to what people say about their felt needs, pressing issues and concerns. See the community from a resident's perspective.
- *Be a good host.* Start a rap-session-type Bible study. Form a neighborhood youth group.

It doesn't happen overnight, but as you become more fully a member of the local community, you will see your credibility with youth increase, and you will have ever greater opportunities to nurture them as disciples.

The Context of Kingdom

A distinction that is sometimes made between the manager and the leader is that the manager knows how to climb mountains, while the leader knows which mountain to climb and why. Details are important, but leaders see the big picture.

The biggest picture this side of heaven is the kingdom of God. What is your relationship to the biggest picture—the kingdom of God—as it exists in the world through Christ's Body, the Church?

The Church's Relation to You: Partner, Supporter and Encourager

Any mission aligned to God's purpose will attract the attention of others in the Body of Christ who share a burden for that purpose. That is why it is important to let others know who you are and what you are doing—to be enriched by their partnership and garner their support.

Ministry requires the *prayers* and *financial support* of God's people. But something else is needed as well.

At the beginning of my journey, I met a ministry leader who was quitting. For two years, he had attempted to do what I was intending to do. He was angry and discouraged; I could "see" his emotional scars. At the end of our conversation, I realized that something else was needed in order to survive the challenges of urban ministry: *encouragement*. I needed people outside the ministry to know what I was experiencing—and to encourage me to persevere in the work.

Urban workers need friends who not only pray and give financially, but who also reach out and touch us with encouragement. We need friends who remind us that we're not alone.

Your Relation to the Church: Point Person, Storyteller

Therefore, since we are surrounded by such a great cloud of witnesses, let us throw off everything that hinders and the sin that so easily entangles. And let us run with perseverance the race marked out for us, fixing our eyes on Jesus (Hebrews 12:1-2a).

As a Christian—especially a Christian leader—you are in great company. "A great cloud of witnesses" surrounds you. Not only do they surround you, but you have also become one of them. Who you are and what you do—in your neighborhood and among the marginalized, the "least of these"—is part of history (His Story), the meta-narrative of the kingdom of God on earth. This context defines your role.

> *Point Person.* You are the point person for a mini-movement of God. You embody the spirit of your ministry: its burden, values and goals. But you are not the totality of your ministry. Everyone on the Hebrews 11 witness list had a supporting cast. They represented something bigger than themselves. You also represent something bigger, just like the witnesses of old.

> *Storyteller.* As you (and, if you have one, your staff) carry out the ministry, one of your most important tasks is to watch for God. "Where is God in all this?" you must constantly ask. You know what He has done (creation, divine imprints) and what He wants to do (salvation, discipleship, animation of potential). So you watch for God's activity in the lives of young people. You take note of comments, questions and responses. You keep an eye out for "aha!" moments. Then you share them—appropriately, without betraying confidences—with friends and supporters. Provide those who pray, give and encourage a window into God's activity within the ministry.

Identity. . . Neighbor. . . Kingdom. A focus on these three elements will position you for maximum effectiveness and future credibility as you pursue the creation of a transformational discipleship ministry.

Note
1. Bobb Biehl, *Leading with Confidence* (Nashville, TN: Aylen Publishing, 2005), p. 36.

Chapter 12

CULTURE

DECODING, MODELING, "HARAMBEE"

was conversing with a colleague who taught leadership classes at our local high school. In passing, he tossed me a compliment:

> "You know Mike [not his real name], don't you? I knew you did! I could tell he's spent time in your ministry . . ."

The flow of conversation kept me from asking, "What tipped you off? How could you tell Mike was a 'product' of our ministry?" But obviously one or more aspects of our transformational discipleship culture had become a part of Mike's way of being in the world.

Cultural norms influence all of us, often in ways we ourselves fail to perceive. I was amazed, after two years of living in Vienna, at my ability to "spot an American a mile away." We really do stand out! Especially American tourists. Tourists from the U.S. convey a confidence that seems almost arrogant. Their stride, in contrast to locals and other visiting foreigners, is strikingly upright, hurried and purposeful. Sometimes their noses actually look as if they are pointing upward! In Vienna, watching was curious fun, but also sobering: *Is that what I looked like two years ago? Is that what I look like now?*

The world we inhabit really does have a squeezing effect on us. That is why the Scriptures warn us to pay attention: "Don't let [Stop allowing] the world around you [to] squeeze you into its own mould . . ." (Romans 12:2, *Phillips*).

The good news is that we can offset the "squeezing" influence of the world with the transforming influence of God: ". . . but let [start allowing] God [to] re-mould your minds from within" (Romans 12:2, *Phillips*).

> Value: Youth programs should be transformational incubators. An incubator is any enclosed structure within which the environment works over time to produce a desired result. Most urban youth ministries already provide places of safety, fun and learning for inner-city kids. They can do more. They can foster transformation.

Thinking and Apprenticing

There were two activities instrumental in Jesus' ministry that tend to be undervalued today. The first was His approach to discipleship: He *apprenticed.* He asked His disciples to follow Him—not to memorize facts or take notes in a classroom. They were given a task (to fish for people—i.e., to compel men and women to enter the kingdom of God) that involved on-the-spot training. (We have already seen a modern example of the value of an apprentice model of discipleship through Jimmy's story.)

The second activity was one Jesus employed extensively when engaging others: *thinking.* To be more specific, He asked and fielded questions. About 20 years ago, I heard a quotation—attributed to well-known Bible teacher Cyril J. Barber—that went something like this:

> Jesus used *questions* throughout his ministry; He used *questions* to begin a conversation (John 5:6). He reasoned

with *questions* (Matthew 12:24-30). He taught with *questions* (Matthew 18:12). After telling the crowd the story of the Good Samaritan, He asked, "Which of the people in the story do you think proved to be a neighbor to the man who fell into the hands of the robbers?" (Luke 10:36). On another occasion when the religious leaders tried to trap Him with their hostile, incriminating query, the Lord Jesus rebuked them with a *question* (Luke 22:49; Matthew 22:17-21). A great deal of His recorded ministry was conducted by means of *questions*. He used *questions* to hold His listeners' attention and also to stimulate their thought processes.

To ask questions—good, timely, profound questions—requires a measure of skill. To allow others to ask questions of you—probing, searching, honest questions—requires humility, awareness and transparency.

Though they may be generally neglected in our time, these two experiences—*thinking* and *apprenticing*—are defining activities within a transformational discipleship culture. Both require being comfortable with questions.

How do we implement these two methods of discipleship? First, we prepare. Two preparatory activities that foster the leader's capacity to ask and respond effectively to profound questions are decoding and modeling. Second, we create teaching moments. I call these "Harambee" (engaging God and life together) moments.

Decoding

I have addressed at length the life-altering influence of the code of the street on young people. Cultures of brokenness and violence squeeze youth into unhealthy views of God, themselves and others. Important, therefore, to creating an environment of transformational discipleship is the practice of *decoding*.

The dictionary defines "decoding" as converting a secret message—often a set of letters, numbers or symbols—into words that can be understood.[1] To decode is to uncover an underlying meaning. For our purposes, decoding is the practice of excavating central ideas (the youths' and God's) in order to accentuate God's perspective in the minds of young people.

In editor Walter Hooper's preface to *God in the Dock: Essays on Theology and Ethics*, he describes C. S. Lewis's motivation for translating the gospel into common language:

> After his conversion in 1931, Lewis, who seldom refused an invitation to speak or write about the Faith, found himself moving in very different circles. He preached to and argued with fellow dons, industrial workers, members of the Royal Air Force, and university students. It was partly due to this varied experience that he came to see why the professional theologians could not make Christianity understandable to most people. As a result, he set himself the task of "translating" the Gospel into language which men use and understand. He believed that if you found it difficult to answer questions from men of different trades it was probably because "You haven't really thought it out; not to the end; not to 'the absolute ruddy end'."[2]

I inadvertently began decoding while attending seminary in Colorado. Theological concepts using words with ten letters or more rarely enter normal conversations. So I played a game during the 25-minute drive from the campus to my home. "If I had to explain this concept to the kids tonight, how would I do it? What would I say?" I would challenge myself to translate—decode—complex concepts into terms youth would understand.

Finding Core Ideas

For years, in addition to running Neighborhood Ministries, I served as a teaching pastor. That meant decoding ideas coming from two directions—the Scriptures and the youth—on a regular basis. With the Scriptures, I learned to search for theological centers. To know what a passage *means*, one must first discover what it *meant*. Someone once said, "If you know what the biblical writer is saying and what the biblical reader is hearing, you can know what God is saying." Surfacing the core ideas of biblical texts is key to persuasive preaching.

With youth, getting at the heart of what they are saying requires listening and probing without bias or presumption. Author Stephen Covey famously said, "Seek first to understand, then to be understood." Group discussions are as much about listening as they are about speaking. So the youth leader must probe:

"What do you mean by that?"
"Finish your thought . . ."
"Why do you think that?"
"Help me understand . . ."

Injected throughout is the clarifier: "So is *this* what you are saying?" This lets youth know that you are listening, and that you desire to understand. It also allows you to summarize their thoughts.

This is a significant decoding moment: You are hearing youths' thoughts on life in their own words. Summarizing their thoughts may or may not reveal new ideas regarding youth perspectives. But by putting central ideas in terms they have expressed, key concepts will come across as fresh, perhaps new, to *them*. Later, when applying God's perspective, it will be as if God is speaking directly to them.

The search for central ideas is a difficult task. It is easy to follow the practice of the pagans of Jesus' day, who equated wordiness and repetition with spiritual persuasiveness (see Matthew 6:7).

Thoughts are much more powerful when they are focused. This requires mining for single ideas. Haddon Robinson, in his book *Biblical Preaching*, highlights this truth:

> *Students of public speaking and preaching have argued for centuries that effective communication demands a single theme.* Rhetoricians hold to this so strongly that virtually every textbook devotes some space to a treatment of the principle. Terminology may vary—central idea, proposition, theme, thesis statement, main thought—but the concept is the same: an effective speech "centers on one specific thing, a central idea."[3]

Deriving central ideas from youth can be as simple as summarizing the points youth make during a discussion. "Johnny, you said your mom is always breaking promises, which makes you feel it's alright to disobey her. Tasha, you expressed fear and anger about the possibility that your parents might break up. It sounds like all of you wish you had a *better relationship with your parents* [their core issue, which also is a felt need]."

Your response might be based on Paul's exhortation to children to honor their parents (see Ephesians 6:1-3) and could include some or all of the following: "This is not about your parents; this is about you." "You respect your parents, not because they deserve it, but because it is the right thing to do." "You did not choose your parents, but how you respond to them is your choice." "Ask why they are the way they are; examine your responses as well." "It won't be easy, but if you honor them (i.e., look up to them and appreciate the good in them) and love them (i.e., seek that which is best for them), the negative stuff won't hurt you. You can work your way through it."

Youth leaders are not preachers, per se. But, like preachers, we are tasked to persuade our audience—which in our case happens to be youth. Persuasive ministry requires knowledge of the audience's view of the world and God's view of the audience. This means decoding.

Modeling

I once took a youth group to Red Rocks—a huge outdoor amphitheater in the foothills of Golden, Colorado. The amphitheater sits between two very high rock formations. As we stood atop the theater, we noticed that some people had climbed to the top of one of the formations—a very dangerous and illegal act.

Glaring at the climbers, I shouted in disgust, "What a dangerous and stupid thing to do!" Then, as we walked away, I muttered to myself, "I hope they'll be okay."

One of the kids heard me. "How can you say that?" she asked. "Why would you care about what stupid people do?"

That was when I first realized that others were sizing me up. And they weren't afraid to question what they saw.

We are being watched all the time. The ability to bear up under such scrutiny is an important part of the transformational discipleship environment.

Life in a Glass House

One of the first things I was told about being a missionary was that missionaries—even missionaries in the inner city—live in glass houses. I took that to mean that people who serve God lead transparent lives.

Much is made today of the difference between our inner and outer selves. While this distinction has some merit, an unintended consequence can be the affirmation of duality as a way of life.

This is not God's way. The inner and outer lives of the disciple are to be consistently shaped by God's Spirit and instruction. We return to Paul's exhortation: "Do not conform to the pattern of this world, but be transformed by the renewing of your mind. Then you will be able to test and approve what God's will is—his good, pleasing and perfect will" (Romans 12:2).

Transformation should produce behaviors consistent with beliefs. Youth leaders should be comfortable living under the scrutinizing lens of discerning youth. What young people see in us should reinforce what we say about following Christ, whether it is what we preach on Sunday, what we tell someone in a personal conversation, or the day-to-day acts of our lives that whisper our true convictions.

What You Whisper

Years ago I took a Christian writing class from Dr. Bruce Shelley at Denver Seminary. Dr. Shelley made many profound statements, not the least of which was: "In writing, it's not just what you shout, but what you whisper!"

I have since learned to appreciate the beauty of the implied. The Old Testament book of Esther is fascinating for this very reason: God is never mentioned by name, yet His presence fills the narrative. Powerful affirmations or damning contradictions can spring from that which is subtly implied.

The concept of whispering occurs in realms other than writing. Think of a child in a room filled with adults. What draws that child to one adult over another? They sense what is whispered: "You can entrust yourself to me."

What do you whisper? Sadly, a great many politicians whisper dishonesty while shouting sincerity. Those who direct transformational discipleship ministries must live lives of integrity—down to the whispers.

You Matter

There is an indispensable element in all this: you. Unless you, as the leader, model what you teach, you cannot create a transformational discipleship culture.

I won't lie; this is a costly standard. A commitment to modeling places a number of demands on leaders' personal lives:

- Leaders examine their lives: they watch their lives and doctrine carefully (see 1 Tim. 4:16).

- Leaders walk with God: they live lives of obedience and devotion.
- Leaders apply what they teach (James: "You who say do not steal—do you steal?"): they allow the Holy Spirit to apply lessons first *to* them and then *through* them.
- Leaders are transparent: they share their journey with others.
- Leaders stay freshly attuned to God: they study the Scriptures again and again as if for the first time.
- Leaders model a God-shaped purpose: they live purpose-driven lives.
- Leaders model love: they seek only the highest good of others.

Harambee Moments

The term "Harambee" has a rich African history. In 1964, one year after its declaration of independence from British rule, the Republic of Kenya was born. Its president, "Mzee" Jomo Kenyatta, based his mandate in something that would become a motto for the people of Kenya: Harambee (which in Swahili means "let's pull together!" or "pulling all together at once"). Later adopted by many ministries in the West, the term captures a sense of striving together toward a desired goal.

While the adolescent leadership program is the central *activity* of a transformational discipleship ministry, Harambee is its central *event*. A significant part of every youth gathering is (or should be) when young people come together for a time of discussion and a short talk about God. This is what I call the Harambee moment.

It's club night. About 25 middle school-aged youth are mingling, waiting for club to start. Above the chatter, Karen speaks:

Okay, here's the situation. Sondra—this is a made-up story—gets into a fight with Jessica at school. No one sees who started it, but everyone knows it *had* to be Jessica. Sondra *had* to be just defending herself. Both girls get suspended from school. Is that *unfair* [she points to one side of the room] or *fair* [pointing to the other side]? You make your choice . . .

Gradually kids start to move. Kids on the "fair" side slowly notice that only one person—Carl—is walking toward the "unfair" side of the room. When Carl turns around, he is surprised to see the rest of the group laughing and pointing at him. After the initial shock, he smiles and shrugs his shoulders. During discussion time:

Karen: Carl, why did you think suspending both of them was unfair?

Carl: It's wrong for two people to get punished when only one of them deserves it.

Tonya: But you don't know who started it.

Niles: Maybe they should have investigated it more.

Carl: Hey, I know what it's like to get punished for something I did not do. It's just not right.

Later, Karen gives a wrap-up:

We have all been accused of doing something we did not do. We may have even been punished for it. And, Carl, you're right: that's wrong.

But what can you do about it? It's not like you can argue your case in court. Schools aren't set up for that kind of thing.

Jesus talks about this, but you may not like what He says. In His day, people were taught to settle arguments by doing to others what they do to you. "You have heard it said," Jesus told a crowd, "Eye for eye, tooth for tooth." They were taught if someone hits you, you hit back!

Jesus says people who follow Him respond differently. He says, "But I say to you: Do not resist an evil person." Don't resist? What's up with that?

[Karen holds up a poster.] You see this picture? Two middle-aged women, one black and the other white, standing arm-in-arm, smiling. They're friends. Now look at the smaller picture in the corner. See that black girl wearing the shades? She's walking into a school that, for the first time, has been ordered by law to allow black students to attend. You see the crowd of white people? They're angry! They don't want black people in their all-white school!

Now look closely at the white girl towards the front of the crowd who's screaming. Recognize her? She's the same person who is hugging the black woman. Now look closely at the black girl wearing the shades. See who she is? That's right: she's the black woman in the large picture!

The white girl hated black people. She screamed at them. But the black kids did not scream back. And later the black and white women became friends.

But when Jesus said, "Do not resist an evil person," He was not just pointing to behavior. He was pointing to the necessity of a transformed life.

Jesus knew that no one could resist evil for very long. If a person keeps pushing your buttons (nags you, calls you names, gets in your face), at some point the best of us will snap.

That was Jesus' point. You can't resist, at least not on your own. But if Jesus is in your life, you will. Why? Because *Jesus removes the buttons other people push in order to hurt and control you.*

What if someone wants to pick a fight? How would they do that? Would they call you a name? Would they call your mother a name? ("Yo mama!" is a phrase that has provoked many a fight!) They're looking for a button—something you're sensitive about—to get you angry enough to fight. But what if there is no button to push? What if you are so secure in your (and your mother's) self-worth that any provocation sounds like nonsense? That's what Jesus does: Those who belong to Him discover who they really are. And when you know who you are, no one can bait or hurt you. There are no buttons to push.

So, going back to Jessica and Sondra, God shows up (or wants to show up) before the fight begins. If it is on you, you won't pick a fight with anyone because, like Jesus, it is not in your nature to do so. If someone wants to pick a fight with you, they will fail because you are not someone who can be provoked.

Make sense? This week think about the buttons people push to make you angry. What needs to change in you in order to remove that button? I challenge you to ask God to make that change in your life. Let's pray . . .

I think of Harambee moments as times with the "multitude." While Jesus spent significant time with the 12 disciples, He often addressed large crowds of people who were following Him. To these multitudes He said repeatedly, "Whoever has ears to hear, let them hear."

The multitude was filled with different kinds of people. There were those who believed Jesus' message. There were curious onlookers. There were "groupies" who did not take Jesus' words seriously but thought it cool to be part of the crowd. To this diverse group of people, He spoke truth, with the exhortation and plea: *"Whoever has ears to hear, let them hear."*

Your "multitude" might be your basketball squad, intermediate dance studio or weekly club attendees. No matter what brings them together, they are diverse in terms of their relationship with, understanding of and/or commitment to God. It is to this group that you bring the Harambee moment.

It is important to understand the context you are creating. Harambee is a focused time of engagement around a felt need. We are "scratching where the youth are itching." Our goal is to present God's perspective in a way that touches the group's felt need.

- This is not a time for hanging out or basking in the moment of being with kids. You may be facilitating, and you certainly are in charge. But this moment is not about you. Your focus is on the youth. This is your servant leadership moment.
- Time is respected, and timeframes adhered to. For Harambee moments to be impactful, time must be used carefully. We are not cavalier about time, like the proverbial preacher who could have stopped 30 minutes ago but did not. (Once, before speaking for Denver Seminary's Chapel service, John Perkins asked how much time he had. "Take all the time you need." Dr. Grounds replied. "But when you're finished: *stop*.") Better to stop discussion at a high point than allow for a slow death. If you have not thought through your summary well enough to keep it within five minutes, you have not done your job!
- This is not a time for lecture, but discovery. Topics are introduced creatively, using videos, movie clips or stories taken from yesterday's news. Discussion should be lively: *What do you think, and why?* The only time youth are silent is when you give the wrap-up (a silence earned because you have their respect and your summary is clear and to the point).

Transformational Discipleship and Numbers

You may already have built-in restraints on the number of youth in your program. Many ministries are open-ended: constantly welcoming in new people, hoping they will stay. At times it may feel like a revolving door. This is not a setting conducive to long-term influence.

Two things must happen early on in order for the transformational discipleship culture to take root. First, the group must become comfortable sharing. Then, as sharing grows more transparent and honest, a sense of trust must be established so that the freedom to share continues. You cannot create this safe environment if your youth group is a revolving door for every young person with a passing interest. That may work well within an evangelistic setting, but not in a discipleship one.

Use large group activities during summer months to recruit new kids into your ministry. When the fall program begins, tell them that only those who are faithful attenders through November 1 can continue to meet weekly. After that, if they haven't settled in to regular attendance, they may join in on the monthly fun activities (at full price, of course! They do not get the discount or freebies that faithful attenders get). But they will not be able to participate in the weekly group discussions.

I know this kind of thinking may feel heartbreaking. "But those wayward kids need Christ!" Yes, they do—and so do the young people already committed to the group. Far too many ministries sacrifice kids hungry to learn on the altar of a few not ready to commit.

By November, you will know who you are focused on over the coming year. Staff can now give one-on-one attention to specific youth.

Preparation for Harambee

The Boy Scout motto "Be prepared" applies here. Preparation is key to successful Harambee moments. There are five areas in which preparation must be thorough:

1. *Surface a Need.* Your topic may be "Parents," but what is the felt need? Understanding them? Loving them? Anger towards them? Not having both of them? What is your group's burden—their felt need? Identify what

you perceive to be felt needs, then design discussion questions to draw out any additional felt needs.

2. *Discover the Big Idea.* What is God's perspective? What is His word on the topic? Dig deep enough to discover not only the what but also the why. Then bring the subject (what God is saying) and the complement (what He is saying about what He is saying) into a single, focused, one-sentence statement: the Big Idea.[4]

3. *Choose Your Opener.* It could be a film clip or an interesting statement. Whatever it is, it must be clear, crisp, and draw immediate attention to the topic.

4. *Choose Transitions and Big Idea Illustration.* Transitioning from one segment to the next may be as simple as turning off the projector and asking a provocative question. It could be as short as a three-word command. The important thing is that you have thought it through; transitions must be intentional. You must also select a story that illustrates your Big Idea in a way that helps youth understand and relate to the subject.

5. *Determine an Application.* Give group members something simple to do, such as, "When you get home, tell your parents you love them."

Ministry Incubator

Years ago, a Neighborhood Ministries board member drew a diagram that captured the essence of our ministry. He called it the Sphere of Influence. I do not remember the drawing clearly enough to recreate it, but I do remember thinking it looked like an incubator. That image has stayed with me as I have continued to reflect on our work with urban adolescents.

For every young person entering the world of Neighborhood Ministries, we were an influence for good in some way, shape or form. Not every child embraced the good news of Jesus Christ, but all—through the programs and long-term relationships with staff and volunteers—fell under the influence of God's grace and mercy. Of course, some did find Christ. For them, life in the incubator took on the added dimension of self-discovery and growth as they learned from their Creator who and why they are. When these youth reached high school age, their growth was tested and refined through practical servant leadership opportunities, such as teaching, tutoring, community service—or even running a summer day camp.

The world of transformational discipleship, as I have come to see it, is an incubator. It is built on vision, principles and conviction. It is sustained by the prayers and support of God's people. Its walls are distinctly lined with diverse programs and caring people who provide a constant flow of the love of God into the main chamber.

Inside are kids. They are going through the practical, harsh stuff of life—growing, questioning, changing, hurting, crying, laughing, and so on. They are experiencing life with its ups and downs, its joys and pains. It's hard. But they are not alone. Many caring people have built relationships that provide support structures for them.

That is life in the incubator: people committed to dynamic relationships, walking with youth through life's circumstances over time, with the constant flow of the love of God in the air.

For Love of Culture

Decoding. Modeling. Harambee. These practices will have a character-shaping effect on those exposed to them.

- Young people will feel free to think and express their thoughts. They know that God is not offended or shaken by their honesty. (Remember Job. He pushed back against the judgments of his "friends" with raw honesty, declaring, "I will never admit you are in the right; till I die,

I will not deny my integrity. I will maintain my innocence and never let go of it; my conscience will not reproach me as long as I live" [Job 27:5-6]. God approved Job's honesty [see the end of the book] and vindicated him.)

- There is no "place" where God is "not"—no topic, no discussion, no issue, no felt need. God speaks in hard places to people in hard places.
- It is okay to examine what is going on around you—the way life is squeezing you.
- Integrity matters. Youth should be led by people who can say, "There is nothing you see in me that you cannot become." Youth are drawn to people with integrity.

Notes

1. "Decode" at www.merriam-webster.com, accessed July 2015.
2. C. S. Lewis, *God in the Dock: Essays on Theology and Ethics* (Grand Rapids, MI: William B. Eerdmans Publishing Co., 2014), pp. ix-x.
3. Haddon Robinson, *Biblical Preaching: The Development and Delivery of Expository Messages* (Grand Rapids, MI: Baker Academic, 2001), Kindle edition.
4. For example, consider Ephesians 6:1-3. A study of the passage reveals that Paul assumes children are in the congregation; it is significant that he addresses them directly and not through their parents. Commanding children to obey their parents "in the Lord" reveals an expectation that they will listen to their parents and discern their instructions even as they obey them. In addition, holding their parents in high esteem (simply because they are their parents) brings the promise of a good and long life for them. So if the subject (what he is talking about) is "The wisdom and benefits of obeying parents," and the complement (what he says about what he is talking about) is "It is the right thing to do, and doing so contributes to a good future," the Big Idea might be "The reason God commands you to respect and obey your parents is that this response is the right one, and it yields the promise of a good and long life for you."

Chapter 13

THE INITIATIVE

UNLEASHING LEADERSHIP POTENTIAL

We have come to the component that makes transformational discipleship come alive in the life of the adolescent. It is the creation of a leadership task force: the Emerging Leaders Initiative.

Participants in the Emerging Leaders Initiative are your "Twelve." They are to you what Jesus' disciples were to Him. The Emerging Leaders are the group into which you pour your life. They are apprentices who, in part through your influence, are being prepared to change the world.

Your task is to lead them toward the discovery of their leadership potential. You apply to emerging leaders the exhortation of an ancient Chinese proverb:

Go to the people.
   Live with them.
   Learn from them.
   Love them.
   Start with what they know.
   Build with what they have.
But with the best leaders, when the work is done, the task
   accomplished,
      the people will say:
"We have done this ourselves."

Lao Tzu, Chinese philosopher and poet, 6th century BC

You have lived with the emerging leaders (as a neighbor and mentor), learned from them (through listening and understanding), and loved them (by seeking for them God's best). Now you establish an environment in which they "start with what they know" and "build on what they have." When the ministry year is over, they will look back and marvel at what was done. And they will thank God for it.

The Cohort

Crucial to the success of the Emerging Leaders Initiative is the selection of the "cohort"—the group of young people who will participate as youth leaders. The Initiative is not suited for everyone. Candidates must adhere to the conditions of the program. This might include the expectation that participants will:

- Consistently strive to give as much as they know of themselves to as much as they learn of Jesus Christ.
- Participate as an enthusiastic learner, encourager and cheerleader (not criticize, gossip, or malign peers in any way, but rather pursue their very best).
- Contribute thoughtful interaction, consistent attendance and genuine effort to the cohort team.
- Commit to learning and applying to the best of their ability the disciplines of a life worth living:

  - Prayer: Talking and listening to God
  - Study: Learning about life through God's grid
  - Service: Caring for others, contributing to life
  - Stewardship: Treating all you have as a gift entrusted to you by God
  - Fellowship: Enriching and being enriched by others
  - Fun: Enjoying life and relationships
  - Worship: Honoring God in all areas of life

- Integrity: Living an undivided life
- Respect both elders and peers; seek wisdom from others' life experiences and godly examples; strive to imitate others inasmuch as they imitate Christ.

The Initiative asks a lot of participants, but in return, members of the Initiative receive many rewards, including experiencing the joy and richness of growing their leadership potential. Among other possible outcomes, they will:

- Discover and grow their leadership potential.
- Have fun while engaging in challenging work.
- Receive financial remuneration for their labor (stipends during the school year; salaried employment during the summer).
- Serve kids in their neighborhood.
- Travel to serve children in other cities, on weeklong mission trips to urban areas within and outside the United States.
- Leave behind a legacy of service, as an example other young people can follow.

Cohorts should be small—made up of no more than 6 to 7 people, who together lead a children's group of no more than 35 kids. (You may need multiple cohorts, depending on the size and capacity of your ministry.) Cohorts should be small enough to give members adequate attention, and the ratio of youth leaders to children should be no less than 1 to 5.

Activities

Emerging leaders experience five primary activities over the course of a given year.

1. Influencing Children

Most children's programs consist of a weekly meeting. Each meeting engages in activities appropriate to the age group: crafts, singing, games, etc. There is also a Bible lesson, creatively delivered and designed to capture a child's imagination.

Within the transformational discipleship model, the Emerging Leaders Initiative cohort is the children's program staff. *Each week, a designated teacher is responsible for the selection and arrangement of activities, along with the crafting and delivery of the lesson.* The teacher is the leader. For the first meeting, the Cohort Leader will model (role play) for the cohort how to lead the meeting.

That first week's session should look something like this:

1. Prior to the start of the meeting, you meet briefly with your team to explain the activities, assign responsibilities, and answer any questions regarding the flow of the evening.
2. You explain the lesson you will be teaching and give the staff any special instructions.
3. You allow time for setup.
4. You lead the meeting.
5. Afterwards you gather the staff for a time of debrief/evaluation.

Subsequent meetings will be led by emerging leaders who take turns teaching/leading the children's program.

An important part of training is in crafting the lesson. Do not provide a pre-designed curriculum; rather, teach the youth how to develop their own. Help them brainstorm ideas and themes. Talk about structure, components and flow. Provide resources from which they can glean ideas and find games or other activities. It is important for leaders to learn early on how to design lessons and not be dependent on someone else's work. The Cohort Leader should lead by example, modeling both presentation and the process of design.

2. Learning Together

During the school year, the emerging leaders should meet regularly for times of group study (weekly), fun (monthly) and retreat (in the fall and spring).

Ideally, the weekly study should not take place at the ministry headquarters but in a home. The setting should be warm and comfortable—conducive to honest discussion.

The focus of the study time should rotate among three activities:

- Bible Study. This should include books of the Bible and doctrinal topics, such as faith, salvation, the Trinity, etc.
- Issues. Current events and questions about life should be examined from a biblical perspective.
- Life Study. As awareness of personal capacities and purpose increases, potential adult mentors should be invited to share personal stories and provide wise counsel and advice for those who might wish to follow in their footsteps.

3. Designing the Camp

Emerging leaders are responsible for designing and implementing a month-long summer day camp for third through fifth graders. Accomplishing this task will stretch and add muscle to their already growing leadership potential.

Preparations for the summer program begin in January: setting of dates, official hires/contracts, selecting a camp leader (usually an older emerging leader or local emerging leader graduate). During February through May, the cohort should meet every month for a three-hour training session. The spring weekend retreat should also be a time of preparation. Together the Cohort is responsible for four aspects of the camp:

Theme

The role of the Cohort Leader is to help make the ideas of the emerging leaders come alive, so in January the group chooses a camp theme by brainstorming theme ideas and examining each one in light of the demands of the camp. "If we chose this theme, what would our Learning Center class topics be? Could we develop classes around it? Are there biblical concepts that support it?" These questions evaluate the strengths and weaknesses of each idea, leading the team to the best theme choice.

I remember clearly the process of choosing what turned out to be one of my favorite camp themes: Animal Kingdom: The Wonders of God's Creation. We began at a 6 A.M. group meeting at my house. The discussion went something like this:

"Guys, we need to take some time to decide on a theme for this year's summer camp. Any ideas?"

"How about something related to technology and computers? Kids are fascinated by computers," Johnny piped up.

"That won't appeal to everybody," Danyelle countered.

"What about science?" Danny chimed in. "We could study the natural habitat right around our neighborhood."

"That's a possibility," I responded. "If we choose science, what would our learning center classes look like? Do you think we could come up with Bible lessons that would relate to science?"

"Hey! How about animals?" Levi shouted. "There are all kinds of animals in our neighborhood. And the Bible talks a lot about animals."

"I'm interested in teaching culinary arts. I could come up with learning center classes tying animals to cooking," said Skye.

"I like poetry. I could create classes studying poetry that talks about animals," said Danyelle.

"We could use National Geographic movie clips to illustrate how amazing and unique animals are," Raquel noted.

"It sounds like we're on to something," I concluded.

We all agreed. When we met for our first preparation session in February, we designed the camp around the theme Animal Kingdom: The Wonders of God's Creation.

Content

Once a theme is chosen, it is time to develop the content of the summer program. We generally used a process called—for lack of a better word—"Stickies."

SUMMER ENRICHMENT 2008
Program Planner 1

				Science	Places
Crafts	Music	Games		Art	Writing
Media	Dance	History		Math	_____
Poetry	Animals	Sports		Photography	_____
Field Trip	Cuisine	Books		_____	_____

SEDC08

The Stickies process includes several steps:

- Words describing dimensions of the program (Crafts, Music, History, Places, Media, Poetry, Writing, Field Trips, Animals, Sports, Photography, Cuisine, Books, etc.) are typed on a page, then enlarged to a 36" x 48" sheet, which is taped to the wall.
- The team sits around a table with a stack of Post-its. After a brief discussion, they are instructed to come up with as many ideas related to the theme and components of the camp as they can within 10 minutes. They write them down, one per Post-it. No talking or discussion; this is a 10-minute brain dump. Participants are encouraged to be creative and think outside the box. As they write, the camp leader and Cohort Leader circle the table, collect the Post-its, and arrange them on the sheet.
- At the end of the 10 minutes, each Post-it is read and discussed, and the group decides where it best belongs. That Post-it is then placed on one of two secondary charts.

CAMP COMPONENTS

Components	Stickies/Ideas
Singing	
Bible Lesson	
Group Class	
Group Recreational Activity	
Reading Time	
Electives	
Field Trip	
Craft	
Movie	

SEDC08

LEARNING CENTER CHART

10:00am - 12:00
Monday, Tuesday, Thursday

		Group Session	LC1	LC2	LC3
Week 1	6/18				
	6/19				
	6/21				
Week 2	6/25				
	6/26				
	6/28				
Week 3	CAMPERS @TSTL LEADERS @MISSION TRIP				
Week 4	7/9				
	7/10				
	7/12				
Week 5	7/16				
	7/17				
	7/19				

SEDC08

- By the time this process is finished, the vast majority of the camp's activities will have been drafted. The emerging leaders will have before them a visual snapshot of the "guts" of the camp—and it will all be their design!

Learning Centers

Our experience at Neighborhood Ministries was that after Stickies, the emerging leaders could see where they were going and what needed to be done. Their most important task was to design and teach the Learning Center classes. During the remaining Saturday planning sessions, each staff member would practice teaching their classes to the others, receiving input and advice.

Classroom management was a serious matter: The youth were responsible—from the time the first child entered to the time the last child left—to lead their class. This meant knowing two things: their subject matter and their kids, and they could not accomplish the latter unless they were solid with the former. They all had observed teachers struggling to control their classrooms—most had dished out their share of the grief! Now they were the teachers; what would they do differently to avoid the trouble they knew kids could give them?

Here are a few principles we taught our emerging leaders to help them foster a positive classroom experience—for themselves and for their students:

- Be creative. Choose a theme for your classroom and decorate it accordingly. Design learning stations where kids can focus on differing tasks. Use videos, music, games and crafts. Use nature; use stuff in the community. Keep talking to a minimum. Let instruction be mostly experiential.
- Know how you will start and end each class. Know your transitions. Begin and end on time.

- Pinpoint detractors. Which kid(s) is (are) behaving in such a way as to sabotage your class? Some disrupt loudly, while others do so subversively. Never yell; just point the havoc-makers out to the adult sitting in your class. He or she will escort them out so that your focus remains on teaching the class.
- Have fun! Let your enthusiasm be infectious! Kids should feel when they enter your classroom that they have ventured into your wonderful world, and that it's a great place to be!

Failure to lead the class effectively could have dire consequences, considering—and this was important—no one was going to come to the rescue. I or some other adult might be sitting in the class, reading or doing some work, but our sole responsibility was to be indifferent and do nothing unless asked by those teaching the class. Throughout the training, they were continually reminded, "If you don't thoroughly prepare to lead your class, and if you lose control, they may rise up, tar and feather you, and no one will save you." Classes rotated every 30 minutes, so they would not suffer long, but no one wanted to experience an uprising!

Logistics

Of the four three-hour training sessions, the first was spent designing the contents of the program (the Stickies exercise). The remaining sessions focused on:

- Critiquing learning center classes. Each emerging leader would take a turn teaching while the rest role-played kids in the class.
- Getting special training (e.g., first aid).
- Managing camp logistics: setting up field trips; decorating learning center classrooms; making lists of supplies needed; lining up transportation, meals, volunteers, etc.

A final week of preparation took place during the week immediately prior to the camp. Here we would orient any college interns joining us. (Most ministries recruit college interns to run their programs. Our college interns assisted the emerging leaders.)

Leading the Camp

Summer Enrichment 2007—Week-in-Review

	Monday	Tuesday	Wednesday	Thursday	Friday
	9:00–9:15	BREAKFAST			9:00–9:15
Opening Session 9:15-10:00	9:15 Singing 9:30 Welcome/Announcements 9:40 Bible Lesson	Singing Welcome/Announcements Bible Lesson	Singing Welcome/Announcements Bible Lesson	Singing Welcome/Announcements Bible Lesson	Singing Welcome/Announcements Bible Lesson
Class Time 10:00-12:00	10:00-10:30 Group Class 10:30 - Noon Learning Centers	10:00-10:30 Group Class 10:30 - 12:00 Learning Centers	Field Trip Day	10:00-10:30 Group Class 10:30 - 12:00 Learning Centers	10:00-10:30 Group Class 10:30-11:00 Craft 11:00-12:00 Electives
	LUNCH @ 12:00			LUNCH @ 12:00	
Early Afternoon 1:00-2:30	1:00 Group Rec. Activity 2:00 Reading Time	1:00 Swimming		Swimming	1:00 Group Rec Activity 2:00 Movie Time
Late Afternoon 2:30-4:00	2:30 Electives 3:30 Snack 3:45 Closing Session	Snack Closing Session	Snack Closing Session	Snack Closing Session	Snack Closing Session

There is another way of thinking about the Scout motto "Be prepared." A seminary professor once pointed out to me:

> Why spend hours and years in a practice room studying an instrument? Because one day you will do what for most people is only a dream: perform great masterpieces of musical literature.

The work and preparation of the past year has equipped the emerging leaders to do what other youth can barely imagine: lead a month-long day camp.

In musical terms, they "practiced" during the months of preparation. That is when they worked. Now Day Camp is here, and practice time is over. The time has come to "play."

The ministry leader's primary role now shifts to that of chaplain. Every morning, you lead the staff through a time of devotion and sharing. They can talk about the previous day and encourage one another as they face the new day. Then they take the stage and perform the masterpiece they have been rehearsing.

Take It on the Road

As the saying goes, "You complain you have no shoes, until you meet someone who has no feet." A significant part of the emerging leaders' summer experience is going on a mission trip.

This experience serves two purposes. One is to immerse the youth for a brief time in an environment different from their own. It is especially important that they experience third-world poverty in order to gain a more objective perspective on their neighborhood. A second purpose is to provide opportunities to use their teaching and leadership skills among children in other neighborhoods and cultural contexts.

Youth Development: The Matrix

This is the Emerging Leaders Youth Development Matrix. Each young person is immersed during their high school years in the activities of leadership, discipleship and life study. When finished, they will have experienced growth in the areas of character and wisdom. They will have acquired leadership skills and an awareness of their personal strengths. This will give them a sense of direction as they move toward adulthood. And they will take with them the satisfaction of having influenced for good the generation of young people following them.

As leaders of these emerging leaders, we have the privilege of witnessing transformation in the heart of the city, where youth grow in faith and confidence to serve others, starting with the children of their neighborhood and reaching as far as God's purpose for their lives takes them.

THE
EMERGING LEADERS
INITIATIVE

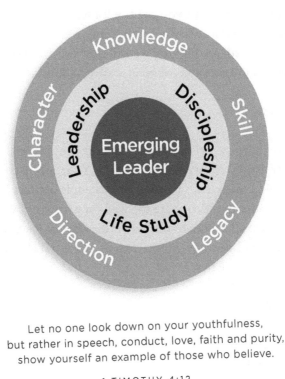

Let no one look down on your youthfulness,
but rather in speech, conduct, love, faith and purity,
show yourself an example of those who believe.

1 TIMOTHY 4:12

Exhortations to an Emerging Leader

You are the leader . . .

It's your class. If you need something, inform the adult sitting in the corner and we will get it for you. If a child is disruptive, ask and your adult partner will remove the child from your class. We will follow your instructions to assist and support you. But you are the leader, and we will not undermine that leadership by rescuing you. Do not worry. Win or lose, succeed or fail, we will be there afterwards to advise and prepare you for greater success tomorrow.

Classroom focus . . .

"Where there is no vision [direction], the people perish [are unrestrained]" (Proverbs 29:18, *KJV*). Your job is to give directional leadership to your class. People are less likely to look sideways if they are focused on what's in front of them. Own your classroom; give it directional leadership, and you will remove 75 percent of potential discipline problems before they start.

Know your role . . .

At any given moment, you are either leading or supporting the leader. You are modeling one of these two roles at all times. Always identify the leader. If you are the leader, lead. We will support you.

Courageous love . . .

How does love (seeking the other person's highest good) impact our response to the problem child? Can we convince them to change their behavior, for their own good as well as the good of the group? If we cannot, or if they are unable to change, do we love them enough to make the tough decision? If our context is not working for them, then let's courageously and lovingly direct them to something better.

Principled leadership . . .

Curriculum, planning, discipline problems, games, leading—where is God in all of this? Must the name of Jesus be spoken for Him to be present? His presence should run deep. God is in the principles and motivations that determine your actions. Jesus is in the details because He is behind the details. Be principled in carrying out your responsibilities. Then when you speak God's name, you give the children you serve something tangible. They will see Him in you, your actions and the program you lead.

Chapter 14

INTEGRITY MATTERS

FORM FOLLOWS FUNCTION

Every organization has its own integrity. To function well, it must abide by its own set of rules.

There are integrity matters associated with transformational discipleship. Of course, there are ethical and moral standards tied to every Christian ministry, but this philosophy of ministry places specific demands upon leaders and organizations. We have covered many of these already. As we come to the end of this book, I want to highlight a few additional challenges faced by those who commit to pursuing transformational discipleship as a way of doing ministry among urban youth.

Handling Discipline Problems

Children at times misbehave. Many an unruly child has disrupted meetings, to his or her delight and to the frustration of leaders and their classes. Sometimes fights that began outside resume and take center stage in your well-planned event! That is when you must address "the discipline problem."

There are aspects to transformational discipleship that minimize this problem. Troublemakers looking for fertile ground may, between September and November, decide not to commit to your program. Additionally, if the ministry is fun, focused and organized, there may not be ample openings to cause trouble.

Generally, the best way to avert discipline problems is through strong directional leadership. Kids focused on what is in front of them have less time to get caught up in side issues or disruptive agendas. Emerging leaders are trained to exert this kind of leadership. But when problems cannot be averted and discipline issues arise, it is time for "Love and Logic."

Years ago, Foster Cline and Jim Fay wrote a book called *Parenting with Love and Logic*. I learned about the concept through personal experience: raising an adopted child. Children who experience deep trauma early in life, whether through abandonment or abuse, will suffer to some degree with attachment disorder. Our family was far from alone in facing this challenge; issues of attachment are extremely common in inner-city neighborhoods.

Foster Cline was a pioneer in the field of attachment disorder. Reading *Parenting with Love and Logic*, I discovered that the principles of raising responsible children and helping the attachment-disordered child were the same. So we adopted a love and logic approach—not only in our home, but also when dealing with the troublesome child in ministry settings.

Keys to Love and Logic

The love and logic approach to dealing with discipline issues fits well with a transformational discipleship philosophy of ministry. Following are a few central principles of this approach to keep in mind:

- No "three strike" rule. Never give a child permission to be disruptive!
- The child is responsible for his or her behavior, not the leader. The leader is, however, responsible for his or her own behavior. Anger and frustration, yelling and arguing, are not appropriate leadership responses—they shift the weight of the problem off the shoulders of the child and onto the leader. The child owns the decision to misbehave. Now he or she owns the consequences.

- Give children choices you can live with. Never give a child a choice you will not be willing to carry out.
- Consequences should be natural, not punitive. The leader should never punish or act out of anger. Your task is to implement a sensible and natural consequence.
- Remember, "You can lead a horse to water, but you cannot make it drink." You cannot force a child to behave. That must be their choice. But your handling of the situation can influence how the unruly child responds.

So when a child gets unruly, we escort them out of the classroom, clarify expectations, and present them with a choice:

> "You know being here requires behaving and listening to the teacher. You seem to be struggling with that. I'm sorry. If you cannot or do not wish to abide by the rules, that's okay, but it means we must send you home. Do you want to abide by the rules and stay, or do you want to go home? Your choice. Which do you want to do?"

This is said calmly, directly and with empathy. If the child chooses to stay, honor that choice and allow them to return to the group. If they mess up again (and many times they will), that is also their choice, so follow through on what you told them before: take them home, inform their parents, and encourage the child to try again next time. Again, there should be no expression of anger or frustration. Because the weight of concern should rest completely on the child, do not bear any of that concern yourself. This is the child's problem—the consequence of their choices.

If the child owns their bad choices, they can also own changing them to good choices. As for the group, the meeting goes on unhindered. And the event sends a message to everyone as to how life works in the children's program.

Adultism

Another integrity issue has to do with adultism. In the world of transformational discipleship, adults play an important role. One role they must *not* play is that of Lord. Especially hazardous to youth leadership development are adults who suffer from adultism: thinking that reaching adulthood gives one the right to lord themselves over adolescents, and that adults are superior to anyone who is not identified as an adult, simply because of their age. Adultism rears its head when adolescents are told, "Do this/Believe this because I said so," or when adults are overly protective and/or controlling.

Such adults will kill youth leadership development. In 1 Timothy 4:12, Paul set the standard: "Don't let anyone look down on you because you are young, but set an example for the believers in speech, in conduct, in love, in faith and in purity." If authority is contingent upon character, adults must exemplify this or lose credibility in the eyes of emerging leaders. Again, in the realm of Kingdom work, stature and authority abide in those who see (and conduct) themselves as servants. For adolescent leadership development to work, adults must embrace the powerful role of experienced life coach.

White DNA

In their book *More Than Equals: Racial Healing for the Sake of the Gospel*, Spencer Perkins and Chris Rice share a painful reality:

> As the smoke cleared after the end of the reconciliation meetings, a survey of the battlefield proved there was a clear victor. The basic conclusion was this: *"Given the fact that white European culture is dominant in this country, given the legacy of racial discrimination that puts whites at an advantage in our society, even in the church, unless we make an intentional effort to affirm black leadership, culture and style, whiteness will always dominate."* This painful realization put racial awareness decisively at the forefront of VOC's [Voice of Calvary's] agenda. There was an

intentional effort to identify black leaders and move them into more positions of influence throughout the ministry ranks and the church.[1] (emphasis added)

When I was pastoring a multiethnic church, we referred to this as "white DNA." We would laugh about it: "You white folks just can't help yourselves, can you?" But it was a painful and serious reality—one that could only be confronted with great intentionality and humility.

Race and class matter. If you are leading an urban ministry, the voices of people indigenous to the population you serve should have influence at every level of your organization. If you are a youth development ministry, your leadership team should consist primarily, if not exclusively, of graduates from your ministry.

The Cost of Integrity

I cannot think of a single ministry that does not, at least by their words, value integrity. Yet real integrity—the kind that permeates an organization at every level—is costly.

- One summer, we had two kids who presented discipline problems. We applied the love and logic approach to both. One changed their behavior and remained at camp. The other, sadly, did not. While we hated to see the child go, we were committed to being people of our word.
- Every summer, college students looking for an urban experience would assist with the day camp. One intern was studying to be an elementary school teacher. She worked with Skye, one of our more experienced emerging leaders. After this intern had persisted in telling Skye what to do, Skye finally looked her in the eyes and said, "Look, I got this." It was a humbling experience for that intern, but through the experience she learned to respect Skye's leadership.

- The decision to bring Jimmy on staff was not without cost. There were people within the organization who disagreed with the move. But it was my decision to make, and it was a decision that was consistent with the purpose of the ministry. So I did it, trusting that this Kingdom investment would bring a return far more valuable than anything I might lose in the process.

The Scriptures place a high premium on integrity. Consider these words from Psalm 15:

> LORD, who may dwell in your sacred tent?
>   Who may live on your holy mountain?
> The one whose walk is blameless,
>   who does what is righteous . . .
> who keeps an oath even when it hurts,
>   and does not change their mind (vv. 1-4).

No Christian organization is perfect. As with an onion, one can peel back the layers of any ministry and find fault. But the nature of transformational discipleship requires a special sensitivity to both walk and talk, values and practice.

The psalmist raises the question, Who may live in God's presence? One requirement is that people who live in God's presence keep their promises.

Every urban youth leader makes a promise ("takes an oath"): to serve the young people within their sphere of ministry. *Building Cathedrals* has examined the substance of that oath. Fulfilling that oath requires a single focus: the pursuit of a ministry marked by integrity.

Note

1. Spencer Perkins and Chris Rice, *More Than Equals: Racial Healing for the Sake of the Gospel* (Downers Grove, IL: InterVarsity Press, 1993), p. 54.

FINAL THOUGHTS

Stories of Transformation

During a recent visit to Denver, Shelly and I had an opportunity to reconnect with Raquel. We had not seen her in a while and were looking forward to getting caught up on events in her life.

It was all we hoped for and more. The child we once knew had blossomed into a beautiful young woman with a budding career as an events planner. Recent challenges had not diminished the qualities that made her special: her smile, her sense of humor, her keen intellect, and her deep love of life.

At one point, Shelly and I shared some of our harder experiences since leaving Denver (we had been gone for four years). As we talked, I noticed that Raquel was *listening*. (Most people are fair listeners, but encountering a good one—someone who weighs your every word, who listens *intently*—can be startling.) After a while she responded: slowly, carefully and lovingly, with empathy, concern and counsel. I found myself on the receiving end of enriching ministry.

As she spoke, memories began to kick in:

I saw a frizzy-haired 16-year-old sitting behind a reception desk. Then the same girl, now 19, is interacting with kids and teens. Then a 20-something version of this young woman is confiding in me: "I don't know if I can do this [lead the summer camp] . . . I'm not a kid person."

"You don't have to be," I reply. "We know you love them ...
you like organizing things ... don't try to be someone you're
not ... utilize your strengths on their behalf."

Powerful memories. Then came another—one that took place
years before Raquel's time:

A young believer in his twenties is walking with his pastor.
"You're leaning on me now," he says, "but the day is coming when we will walk arm-in-arm, serving God together."

I remembered feeling excited, looking forward to that day.
Raquel was still speaking. Turning off the memories, I sat back
and listened. Intently. Drinking in her every word.

At different times over the past few years, Shelly and I have run
into adult versions of kids we once knew:

• We attended a community fundraising event at our
grandkids' elementary school. It was an indoor carnival!
The place was filled with the hustle and bustle of children and family members having a great time. We were
walking down the hall, taking in the excitement, when
two mothers approached me: grown women who were
once girls in our club program. Studying the crowd, I
recognized other parents and adult leaders who had
been involved with Neighborhood Ministries. The setting did not allow for much sharing, but both moms
expressed their appreciation for their Neighborhood
Ministries experience—and hoped their children would
have similar opportunities.

• Shelly and I took our grandkids to the community library. The man at the front desk recognized us. It was
James, one of our original youth group members. He was
a librarian. He shared about his family and the church

they were attending—and expressed gratitude for his experience with Neighborhood Ministries.

- Shelly recently attended Raquel's wedding. (Sadly, I was sick and could not join her.) Two of the young women in the wedding party had, in their teen years, served as emerging leaders. They had graduated from college and were pursuing meaningful careers. They each made a point to express to Shelly how much they appreciated their time at Neighborhood Ministries. They asked her to thank me for the opportunities to travel and develop their leadership skills. (They also promised to pray for my recovery!)

What makes these encounters meaningful is the sense of gratitude that permeates the conversation. We are all grateful—ministry alums and leaders alike—for the influence we had on each other and for the work God did in our lives while we were together.

It would be presumptuous for any ministry to conclude that they are completely responsible (i.e., God's sole channel) for the transformation of a given life. The tapestries of our lives are far too complex for that. God will use a combination of influences that can come from a variety of sources: family, church, school, other ministries, friends, and the like.

But within the scope of God's kingdom agenda, transformational discipleship plays an important role. The biblical principles and divine mandates inherent in the transformational discipleship concept should compel concerned leaders to pursue the infusion of transformational discipleship into the fabric of urban youth ministry.

The rewards that come from *creating environments in which youth can discover who they are in Christ* are many. But I believe the greatest reward is seeing what God has done in an inner-city kid's life, and knowing that you played a role in that transformation.

Transformations like these are needed in city centers across the country and around the world. I believe that urban children and youth hunger for safe, nurturing places in which they can grow into the men and women God has created them to be. And there are people—you, perhaps—who are strategically positioned to create those places and foster that transformation.

> For the urban child hungering to know
>   he/she is fearfully and wonderfully made,
> and for those courageous leaders
>   burdened to see young divine imprints
>   come alive,
> may you discover the joy of igniting potential,
>   transforming young lives, and
>   forging the next generation of urban leaders,
>   all for the glory of God.

For more information about
NEIGHBORHOOD MINISTRIES
visit tdinitiative.org or email
ted@tdinitiative.org

CPSIA information can be obtained
at www.ICGtesting.com
Printed in the USA
LVHW030926240320
651025LV00010B/1186